Grace and Truth;

Under Twelve Different Aspects

Christian Lessons on Being Born Again, the Holy Spirit, God's Forgiveness of Sins, and How to Serve the Lord in Heaven

By William Paton Mackay

Adansonia
Press

Published in 2018

Logo art adapted from work by Bernard Gagnon

ISBN-13: 978-0-359-03011-8

First published in 1872

Contents

Introduction

'The law was given by Moses: grace and truth came by Jesus Christ.' The law showed what man ought to be. Christ showed what man is, and what God is. The law *was given*, but grace and truth came. Calvary tells out fully what man's true state is, what God's truth is, and what grace means. The law is what I ought to be to God: Grace tells what God is for me. The first word of law is 'Thou;' the first of grace is ' God,' so loved; but it is grace through truth. God has investigated everything, nothing has been looked over. The greatest sin that any man could possibly commit has been committed, namely, the murder of God's Son. At the same time the greatest grace of God has been manifested.

Man by nature likes neither grace nor truth. He is satisfied neither with perfect justice nor perfect goodness. If John the Baptist comes in righteousness he is hated, and men say he is too harsh, and not human, but hath a devil. If Christ comes in love. He is taunted with being a friend of sinners. So when the righteous requirements of God's law are preached, many people are apt to turn and say,

'Oh yes, but that is too strict; you must allow a little margin for our imperfection.' God says, make no provision for the flesh. Alas I it will take far too much, but allow it nothing. When a sanctified walk, separated from the world and all its belongings, is insisted on, a certain class are sure to call this legal preaching. And on the other hand when the grace of God is preached, man's wisdom makes it out to be toleration of evil and lawless license.

Let us suppose that a convict, who had just finished his term of penal servitude, wished to lead an honest life. He comes to a man who has a large jewellery establishment, and who requires a night-watchman. He is engaged to watch this house through the quiet hours of the night, when he has everything under him, and every opportunity to rob his employer. On the first evening of his watching he meets one of his old companions, who accosts him, 'What are you doing here?' 'I'm night-watchman.' 'Over this jeweller's shop?' 'Yes.' ' Does he know what you are?' 'No, no, be silent; if he knew, I should be dismissed.' 'Suppose I let it out that you are a re-turned convict.' ' Oh, I pray don't, it would be my last day here, and I wish to be honest.' 'Well, you'll require to give me some money to keep quiet.' 'Very well, but don't let any one know.' Thus the poor man would be in sad fear and trembling, lest it should come to the ears of his employer what his previous character had been. He would be in terror lest he should meet any of his old friends, and lest his resources should be exhausted in keeping them quiet.

Let us suppose, however, that instead of the employer engaging the man in ignorance of his character, he went to the convict's cell and said, ' Now I know you, what you are, and what you've done, every robbery you've committed, and that you are worse than you believe yourself to be. I am to give you a chance to become honest, I'll trust you as my night-watchman over my valuable goods.' The man is faithful at his post. He meets old companion after old companion, who threaten to inform upon him. He asks, 'What will you tell about me?' ' That you were the ringleader of house-breakers.' ' Yes, but my master knows all that better than you do; he knows me better than I know myself.'

Of course this silences them for ever. This latter is grace and truth. The man had been treated in grace, but on the ground that all the truth was out, that his character was known. It is thus God deals with us. He deals in grace, but He knows what He is doing, and with whom He is working, — even the chief of sinners. The whole truth is out about us, and God's grace in the face of this saves, gives a new nature, and puts us down before Himself in the highest places of confidence. Man wonders at this. A wicked companion gets converted, his old associates wonder at his boldness in preaching (like Peter who denied Christ, accusing his Jerusalem hearers of having denied him). They think if his audience only knew what they know, they would be suspicious. God knows us better than we know ourselves, and this is our joy.

Man does not know Grace. When unadulterated grace, unmixed grace, the grace of God, God's own love to sinners, is preached, man cannot take it in. 'Oh, this is downright Antinomianism.' This is the cry that was raised against Luther when he preached 'full free justification by grace through faith without the deeds of the law;' the cry that was raised against Paul, that he made void the law, that he told the people they might sin that grace might abound. Now, unless our Christianity provokes this opposition, it is not scriptural Christianity. Unless the gospel we preach, when presented to the natural mind, brings out these thoughts, it is another gospel than Paul's. Every Christian, mark not some of them, has the Antinomian or God-dishonouring ' flesh,' within him to be watched over and mortified; but this is a different matter. People will readily quote ' Faith without works is dead,' 'We must have works,' and so on; and we most certainly coincide. But follow up the argument by inquiry about the works, and you will too often find that such have very loose ideas of Christian holiness. Such will quite go in for having a Christian name, going religiously to church, being able to criticise a sermon and a preacher, being acquainted with good people, abstaining from all immorality, being honest and respectable; but the moment we cross the boundary line that separates respectable and easy-going make-the-most-of-Christianity, into the rugged, thorny path of identification with a rejected Christ, separation from the world's gaieties, splendours, and ' evil communications,' — dead to it and all that is therein, taking up Christ's yoke, and denying self, — we are met with the expressions, 'too far,' 'pietism,' 'righteous over much,' 'we don't like extremes,' 'legal preaching.'

The *grace of man* would be this, ' Do the best you can by the help of grace, and then wherein you fail grace will step in and make up.' But the first thing the grace of God does is to bring *'salvation,'* (Titus ii. ii,) &c.

Or, again, man's grace may take this shape, ' Oh, yes, we believe in the blood, the precious blood of Christ; only faith can save; and now we have found an easy road to heaven — a sort of short cut in which we can live on good terms with the world and worldly men, and also on first-rate terms with religious men, spend our money to make ourselves comfortable, get a name, honour, or riches here, make ourselves as happy as can be in this world, just take of it what we can enjoy, and go on thus so nicely to heaven.' This is another view of the *grace* that *man* knows about; but the grace of God teaches us that, ' denying ungodliness and worldly lusts, we should live soberly, righteously, and godly in this present world, looking for that blessed hope and the glorious appearing of the great God and our Saviour Jesus Christ' (Titus ii. 12). Thus man knows nothing whatever about the grace of God.

Neither does man know **truth.** He does not know the truth about God. He could quite believe that God made the world, and that he is good to a certain extent; but that God looks upon one sin as making a man guilty as really as ten thousand, he cannot understand. Though written as clear as writing can make it ui the Book of God, he cannot perceive it. Christ brought out the truth about God, that He could by no means clear the guilty, but that he could impute guilt and impute righteousness. An infidel said, ' Is it justice for an innocent man to die for a guilty — is it consistent with reason, either in justice to the innocent or the guilty?' ' Well, suppose it is not, and we may grant it. But what if God became man, and put away sin by the sacrifice of Himself—where is your reasoning now? Our gospel is not an innocent man dying for the guilty merely, but the God-man made sin, and putting it away.' Nor does man know the truth about himself, that he is lost. He thinks that he may be lost, not that he is lost. He hopes, in some vague way, that it will yet be all right with him. Christ brought out the truth about man, that man was hopelessly gone in sin, that he would kill God if he could.

How few there are in *hell* who ever intended to be there! *'Are you to be in heaven?'* Most will answer, *'I hope so.' '* And what right have you *to hope so?*' I once quickly said to a poor woman who looked as like a good person as any of her neighbours. ' If you have believed in the Lord Jesus Christ, why not say so and thank Him, and then begin to hope (not for pardon, there is no such hope in Scripture) for salvation that is to be revealed at perfected redemption and if not, what right have you to have such presumption as hoping to get to heaven when you have not believed in the Lord Jesus Christ'? I saw her some time after, radiant with settled joy and peace, and she said, ' Yes, sir, you asked me what right I had to hope, and I was rather astonished, but I did not take your word about it; I went home to my Bible, and there I found that if I was without God, I had to be without hope in this world' (Eph. ii. 12). This led her to discover ' the sand' on which she had been building, and by God's Spirit she was led to **'the rock.'**

Look at a perfect illustration of grace and truth in the case of the Gentile woman. (Matt. xv. 21-28.)

'*Then* Jesus went thence, and departed into the coasts of Tyre and Sidon.' When? After he had exposed the utter hollowness of man's religion, and the character of the Pharisees' heart. In the beginning of the chapter man brought his religion to Christ, and of course Christ showed that it was the *heart* He dealt with, and not religion.

Verse 8 shows us where the heart of man is — with his religions, his traditions of the elders, his observances, his washing of hands, cups, dishes, tables. It is ' far from God.' Verse 19 shows us *what* his heart has in it: 'Evil thoughts, murders, adulteries, fornications, thefts, false witness, blasphemies.' This is what happens when man comes to God with his religion — with what he has. ' Do you want to know where you are, and what you are?' Bring your religion to God. But Jesus now goes away to where there is no religion, but plenty of misery; no professions, but a great deal of need. He had shown what man's heart has in it—He now wishes to show what is in his heart — a heart that is ' full of grace and truth.'

And behold a woman of Canaan came out of the same coasts, and cried unto him, saying, ' have mercy on me, O Lord, thou Son of David; my daughter is grievously vexed with a devil.' She was a Syrophoenician, a Greek, a Gentile outside of the Jewish territory, a dog in the eyes of every godly Jew. 'Without are dogs.' The dog in the East is not as here domesticated, but is more like a wolf prowling for prey outside the cities — fit emblem of those dwellers by the highways and hedges of Luke xiv., the Gentiles outside the Jewish circle of blessing; and thus we are called 'Gentile dogs.' She had no claim on the 'Son of David.' 'He came to His own.' Her need, her desire, her heart, her faith, were in the right direction; but she must intelligently take the right place in order to be blessed. Her instincts were right; her apprehension of the truth was wrong. This is the reason of that wonderful next word.

'But he answered her not a word.' Many think that this was merely to try her faith — certainly it was; but God accomplishes many ends by one means. He has to manifest not only *grace,* but also *truth.* Had He, as 'Son of David,' blessed her. He would not have kept his true place, for 'He was a minister of the circumcision for the truth of God, to confirm the promises made unto the fathers' (Rom. xv. 8). And she was ' afar off, an alien from the commonwealth of Israel.' He, as Son of David, ' confirmed the promises;' she was a ' stranger from the covenant of promise;' and when she tried that door, she found it righteously shut, because He is faithful and true. He could have no words with her till He got His own and only place in which He could rise above all dispensational thoughts, and let His grace flow forth. Claims of truth had to be settled first, then the fountain of grace could flow; but her need kept her at the footstool. She asked ignorantly, but was in earnest.

And His disciples came and besought Him, saying, 'Send her away; for she crieth after us.' One or other of two courses they might suggest. Peter might have said, 'she is a Gentile dog; she has no right to you as Son of David; send her away.' This would have been *truth*, but at the expense of *grace*; but Jesus was showing grace as well as truth. John might have said, 'She is a poor, needy woman; just give her what she wants, and send her away.' This would have been grace, but at the expense of truth. Now Jesus was showing truth as well as grace. This is so like man — he cares for little but his own comfort. ' She crieth after us.' 'Us' always must be consulted. How unlike Him who gave ' Himself for us,' when He came as grace and truth. 'What does it matter about dispensational truths, if sinners are saved?' Such is man's talk—and it matters little to the sinner; but what of God's claims and God's truth? ' We do not study this or that truth because it is not essential.' Essential to you or to God? The disciples could not harmonize grace and truth, and therefore they had to sacrifice the one or the other, but both are to be seen. Man would earlier repel from God as an angry Judge, and give no good news to any sinner, or He would undermine the pillars of His throne by giving universal salvation; but ' grace and truth came by Jesus Christ.' He now takes occasion from the appeal of the disciples to let out a little of His mind.

But he answered and said, ' I am not sent but unto the lost sheep of the house of Israel.' As ' Son of David,' He keeps by His peculiar mission. She does not belong to the lost sheep of Israel's house; how, therefore can He speak to her or grant her the request she presented? He could not deal as ' Son of David' with a Gentile, because she was not of the house of Israel. Was this not truth, some would even think, to harshness? But this is man's idea of harshness. God's truth is never harsh. Grace without truth is sentimentality. Truth without grace is harshness. All this is only (not to ' send her away,' as was the disciples' easy method, but) to lead her to give

Him His true place, and then to take her own true place in which grace could flow to her. Why are we not blessed with God's grace? He is waiting to be gracious. How long will He wait? Till we give Him His true place, and till we take our true place before Him, where He can bless us. When he speaks, she listens, and now takes up her request again.

Then came she and worshipped, saying, ' Lord, help me.' She did not say she was as good as Israel's lost sheep; but she leaves out the title ' Son of David,' and calls Him Lord. ' If He is but sent to Israel's lost sheep, I can't call Him Son of David, and be blessed; but He has another and a higher sovereign name, and that is Lord Jehovah, who can help even me. He won't break down the dispensational wall that keeps the poor Gentile dog away from the promises of the Son of David; but He can rise above it in a power that can reach down to help and succour me.' She gives Him now His true place. This is seen in her not using the title 'Son of David,' but only that one word ' Lord,' His true name to her as a Gentile. ' They that know Thy name will put their trust in Thee.' But she had not quite reached her own true place. She needed something more than help -, but Jesus, now addressed as Lord alone, can speak to her and reveal a little more. She listens, believes, and always takes up at each step the thought of the fresh revelation, the words that dropped from His lips, for she was in earnest.

But He answered and said, ' It is not meet to take the children's bread, and to cast it to the dogs.' Here is her name; is she prepared to take it, as well as give Him His? Well might she have said, ' Me a dog, forsooth! I know many so called children of Israel who make a greater profession, and I would not be seen with them.' This would have been natural. When man does not feel his need, he compares himself with others. He vindicates, excuses, palliates himself—'Many make more profession than I do; yet I would be ashamed to do what they do.' Very possibly; that is their business; but what of God's claims on you? She felt that her need was deep, and her answer is according to it She takes the place the Lord gives her, not what she would choose, but what He indicates.

And she said, ' Truth, Lord. Yet the dogs eat the crumbs which fall from their master's table.' This is the place of power. This is the place of blessing.

1st. 'Truth, Lord.' Any name you please — 'a sinner,' 'a dog;' but

2d. If I am a dog, it shall be at your table; and there I'll claim the dog's portion. ' Yet the dogs eat the crumbs.'

We take the guilty sinner's name,
The guilty sinner's Saviour claim.

I am a great sinner I ' Truth, Lord;' yet the great sinner claims the great Saviour. I am the chief of sinners! ' Truth, Lord;' yet the chief of sinners claims the chief of Saviours. I am ignorant I ' Truth, Lord; ' yet Christ is my wisdom. I am unrighteous! 'Truth, Lord;' yet Christ is my righteousness. I am unholy! ' Truth, Lord;' yet Christ is my sanctification. I am in bondage! 'Truth Lord;' yet Christ is my redemption. That 'yet' is the pleading of need from the place that truth has given.

Mercy and truth are met together;
Righteousness and peace have kissed each other.

And now what is the answer, and what was the result?

Then Jesus answered and said unto her, 'O woman, great is thy faith; be it unto thee even as thou wilt.' This was the answer, the very resources of Jehovah thrown open for her use. ' And her daughter was made whole from that hour.' And this was the result, 'From that hour.' What hour? The hour in which she said, 'Truth, Lord.' The hour in which she took the dog's place, and claimed the dog's portion. Is this but a crumb from His blessed table? What must the full feast be, when the Church of God, gathered out of Jew and Gentile, shall sit down at the marriage supper as the bride of the Lamb; and every prayer shall have ended, because all have been answered; and the combined glory of grace and truth shall shine out for ever from the brows of all the myriads of sinners, saved by grace, who came in all their degradation and need to the feet of Jesus, giving Him His true place, and taking their true place? Friend, God now waits to be gracious to you; but you must take the dog's place.

In the following papers I have tried to preserve the balance between grace and truth. ' The grace of God' brings salvation, this is the truth of Titus ii. ' The righteousness of God ' — God being just and justifying Him that believes in Jesus, — is the truth of Rom. iii. I have endeavored to show the grace and truth of God: —

1st. With regard to the justification of a sinner. Grace has to be seen and truth seen, each equal to the other.

2d. With regard to the sanctification or growth in grace of a believer. Grace is seen and truth is seen. 'Being made free from sin and becoming servants to God ye have your fruit unto holiness, and the end everlasting life,' Rom. Vi. 22.

I will here give the thread on which the papers in this volume are crystallized: —

1st. ' *There is no difference,*' for until a man sees this, he is not in the place where God can bless him. This is fundamental.

2nd. *Would you like to be saved?* 'Whosoever will' is pointed to the work of Christ for sinners.

3rd. '*Ye must be born again*' — Wherein are discussed the necessity and nature of regeneration. Regeneration is an act done at the same time as justification — not a work, as many seem to think, confounding it with gradual sanctification. Justification gives pardon and acceptance. Regeneration gives a new life, a new nature at the same time perfect in parts but not in development, sanctification being the development of this new life. In this is discussed the question what is the water of which we must be born again?

4th. *Do you feel your sins forgiven?* In this is pointed out that most dangerous error of confounding man's feelings with the testimony of God's word — the confounding of the eighth chapter of Romans with the fifth — the confounding of the Spirit's witness to sonship with ' Being justified by faith we have peace with God ' — that we stand only on the written word ' Thus saith the Lord' for our ' knowledge of salvation,' as we stand only on the incarnate Word for that salvation itself.

5th. *The work of the Holy Spirit.* The connection and difference between the work of the Spirit in me and Christ's work for me are here considered. Many souls would wish to study the work of the Spirit in them first, but only a saved man can profitably study this; one who has come through the former chapter, ' Do you feel your sins forgiven.' The Holy Ghost is never mentioned in Romans till the fifth chapter. Misplaced truth is the worst error.

6th. *'Heaven opened.'* In which we get a glimpse of the counsels of God in the past, present, and future. Heaven is opened now for us and all that is there is ours. The epistle to the Hebrews discloses our opened heaven.

7th. *Triumph and conflict* come next. The conflict before was between me and God, now it is between me and myself, and this will be a life-long conflict, for every Christian is in the world, has the flesh within and Satan against! him. These are typified by Israel in Egypt, which is spiritually the world —in the Wilderness, where Amalek (the *flesh*) has to be defeated — and in Canaan, where the Canaanites (*'spiritual wickednesses'*) have to be overcome. That' Satanic trinity' is considered in the three following papers in detail.

8th. *Under the sun.'* Our great foe 'the world' is here j looked at. What is it, and how is it to be overcome?

9th. *'No confidence in the flesh'* — the believer's beacon-dre. Here we consider what true holiness is and what it is not. Not the old nature made better, but the believer as a whole, as an individual, made better by his new nature keeping the old under. In this is shown the all-important ' truth concerning the existence in the one individual saved man of two distinct natures. The one person has two natures, one that cannot sin because born of God, the other that cannot but sin because born of Satan. Our practical holiness does not consist in assimilation, but in opposition — not in improvement of the old man, but in his mortification. Our responsibility remains in the individual person, possessed of these two natures.

10th. *The devil.* The truth so plainly shown in Scripture concerning the real personal existence, and not mere influence of the devil; where he is, what he is doing, and our power over him are stated.

11th. *'Serving the Lord'* now comes in, since we are made free from our foes, since our bands are loosened, we can now serve. 'Let my people go that they may serve me.'

12th. *Judgment* is looked at as past with regard to the believer's person, present as to the believer's ways, and to come for the believer's works. Many Christians fail to see the perfect balance here between grace and truth — grace putting us for ever beyond judgment, and truth bringing up at the judgment seat of Christ all our deeds done in the body, good or bad.

In issuing a new edition, we would merely record our adoring thanks to Him whose name is Wonderful, for having in any way used these pages as the means, of sending.: light into dark hearts, or of solving difficulties to those who already knew His grace and truth, and leading them more intelligently to walk with Himself.

May the gracious Spirit whose it is to lead into all truth bless what is His own in these pages, to the glory of the ever blessed Lord Jesus Christ, our God and Saviour.

W. P. M.
Springbank, Hull,

There is no Difference

Our Condemnation

YOU are always preaching and writing that the vilest and most unworthy are welcome to come to Christ; but what of those that do not feel so very vile?' a sister in the Lord once said to me. This is a most important question, in regard to a class of people very difficult to reach.

She told me that a friend, after having heard a preacher of the gospel describing the awful state of unsaved people, and giving a solemn exhortation to be saved immediately, said, with great surprise, *'But what is it all about? I feel as happy as a bird.'* She really could not understand that anything the man had been saying had any reference to her.

Such people never did anything very bad. They have been trained up under all the influences of a Christianized society. They never knew vice in its open nakedness. They never felt anything at all very evil in their hearts. They have never been face to face with God, nor taken God's idea of sin. In short, they know not the God revealed in Scripture. I do not mean that they are idolaters or infidels in the popular sense of these words. They know a god that is a sort of being for pulpit use, a being that is to be addressed as a matter of course, and religious duty, at times of particular solemnity. They have a few ideas, derived from various sources, of a being called God, but of the God of Holy Scripture they have no conception. The God who judges sinners they do not know; of God's estimate of sin they have never heard.

But let me be distinctly understood as to this most important matter. Let us imagine a man wandering on the top of some high cliffs. A bright warm sun is overhead, and a soft green carpet of grass is beneath his feet. He feels very happy and gay, but he is going nearer to an awful precipice I He is happy, but he is blind. We call, we shout to him to stop. He turns round and says, *'What is it all about? I feel as happy as a bird;'* but onward still he goes. Would it not be love on our part to go and take hold of him, and earnestly tell him that a fearful precipice lies a yard before him?

Dear friend, this is where we see you. I have in my mind at this moment an accomplished young lady, amiable, kind, and dutiful, surrounded by all that can make life happy; one who has her neat Bible or Prayer-book, and who is seen most regularly and religiously in her seat in church or chapel every Lord's-day, who takes great interest in deeds of charity, visits the poor, and is very happy. No one ever dared to say to such an one, 'You are on the broad road that leadeth to destruction.' It would be considered highly improper so to do. Perhaps this silent page may be before your eye, and now it would say to you what has been so long unsaid, 'Stop! are you ready to meet God? where shall you spend eternity?' If you were separated this moment from all the dear friends around you, and all those happy scenes, and that comfortable home, and standing before God, what have you to say? I wish to write a little of what He thinks of you. I am not to write about what your parents, your friends, your pastor, or spiritual adviser think of you. They may think most highly of you, and most justly too, as you may be everything that could be desired from a human point of view. But I wish to place before you what God your Maker thinks of you; yes, of you yourself, whoever you may be; the more refined, cultivated, educated, and wealthy, the more would I be in earnest to get your attention. You may be a princess or an empress, but one word expresses God's estimate of you, and that word is — 'sinner.'

A rich lady one day, when she heard a person speaking of all as sinners, said with great surprise, —

'But ladies are not sinners!'

'Then who are?' she was asked.

'Just young men in their foolish days.'

I have not the slightest doubt but that this is a very common idea, though seldom expressed. A lady who had heard some one preaching this kind of truth called on him and said,—

' Do you mean to say that I must be saved just as my footman? '

' Most certainly.'

' Then I shan't be saved.' Poor lady I that was her business, and this was her fatal decision. My reader, I not only wish to tell you that *you* are a *sinner* —you, educated, amiable lady — but that in God's sight you are just the same as the vilest profligate; just the same as that man you heard about who was hanged for murdering his wife This is most terrible, but it is true. I remember once saying it to a young man who was not like you, but who knew that he was very bad; and he said,—

'I believe all are sinners, but I don't believe that all are the same.'

' Well, we have only one authority to refer to, and it is within your reach; will you take your Bible, and remember one thing, that it is God who speaks. Turn now to Romans, the 3rd chapter and 22d verse, and at the last clause we read, "*For there is no difference*; for all have sinned, and come short of the glory of God." This is what God has said.'

' Well,' said my friend, ' I never saw that before.'

' But it was there although you never saw it.'

And now, dear reader, you who are happy and amiable, this is the one thing I wish to tell you from God, *'There is no difference.'* This is what you never could and never can feel; it is a thing for which you must believe God. As it is God with whom you have to do, I beseech you do not listen one moment to any that would take you from His truth. *He says* 'there is no difference; ' He has proved that the lawless Gentile or heathen and the law-breaking Jew or religious person are equally guilty, and that not one among either the outwardly profane or the outwardly decent is found righteous or good before Him. Of course there are differences in heinousness or degradation of sins. I need not stop to speak of this; we all know it. I wish to tell you what you and I do not by nature know; namely, that there is no difference as to where we stand before God. The one question is, guilty or not guilty. There are no degrees as to the fact of guilt. '   He that offends in all points is guilty of all,' and nothing less. He that offends in all points is guilty of all, and nothing more. Therefore, while there are differences among offences, there is no difference as to guilt. Therefore, all men in the world (and you included), have been brought in guilty before God.

Look at the story of the Prodigal Son in the 15th of Luke. The moment he crossed his father's threshold with his pockets full of money and a respectable dress on, he was as really guilty, as really a sinner, as when he was among the swine in his rags. He was more degraded when keeping swine, but not more guilty. In fact, his degradation and husks were his greatest mercies, for these led him to see his guilt. A full pocket and a respectable appearance are the worst things a guilty sinner can have, as these lead him to think that he is rich and increased with goods, and has need of nothing, when in God's sight he is wretched, and miserable, and poor, and blind, and naked. I do not ask you, Are you a sinner in the common use of that word? because you for whom I write are not. You mean by sinner, one who is very wild, profane, disobedient, and lawless. This is as men speak of sinners. God, however, says that there is no difference. The only thing I ask you is this. 'Have you offended in one point— not one point of open sin, but one point in thought or word.' You confess to at least one point. God asks no more. If you have offended in one point you are guilty of all, Man would never think this nor say it. But God says it. Suppose that your life were like a book that you have written, and there was only one small blot just like a pin's-point in it, whilst all the other leaves were perfectly clean, and you came and presented it before God; He would put it beside all the blackest lives that ever lived, the blackest histories of the vilest murderers, and thieves, and harlots, and over this collection would be written these words,

'There is no difference.'

You have offended in one point. It is not a question of being a great sinner — it is this question,

' Are you perfect: as the Christ of God, the perfect man?' If you had lived for fifty years without committing one sin, or having one wrong wish or thought, and just then you had an evil thought, and afterwards lived another fifty 3'ears and died, aged one hundred, with only this one evil thought (not even a word or an action), when you came to stand before God in judgment. He would put you beside all the offscourings of the earth, men who for a hundred years never had a good thought, and He would say, 'There is no difference.'

Of course you would think this is very hard, but it is true. God will never ask your opinion whether it ought to be so or not. He has in grace told us already what He will do. You and I, not knowing absolute holiness, cannot understand or appreciate such a judgment. We could never feel that every one is the same in God's sight as regards guilt. But God says it, and there the matter ends. If you wish to go on, risking your chance of escaping hell on the possibility that God has told lies, and that these words are not perhaps quite true, that ' there is no difference' then the judgment-day will declare it to you. I would rather advise you to believe God, against your own ideas and opinions, and simply because He has said it, to proceed as if in His sight, ' there is no difference' between those we call great and little sinners.

'I cannot believe that all are so bad,' said one, after I had been saying 'there is no difference.'

' But,' I added, ' the Bible says, "there is no difference."

' But there must be greater sinners than others.' ' Oh, yes. Most certainly. Great offenders are recognized in the Bible; he that owed fifty and he that owed five hundred pence; but as to guilt, God says, "there is no difference."'

'*Well, I cannot see it,*' still continued my friend.

'*But it is in God's Word, whether you see it or not*; ' and it is sufficient that God has said it, for His Word is truth. Let me give an illustration. Let us suppose that a bill had been stuck up in this town, saying that recruits were wanted for Her Majesty's Life Guards, and that none would be enlisted but those who were tall and measured not under six feet in height. Let us suppose that many of the young men in the town were anxious to serve in this regiment, and John meets fames, and says to him, 'Well, I've more chance than you, for I am taller than you;' and they put back to back and measure themselves with one another, and indeed John is taller than James. And there continues to be much measuring in the town before the day that the recruiting-sergeant comes.

They measure themselves by themselves, and compare themselves among themselves, but they forget one thing — that not only tall men, but men not under six feet are wanted. One man at last says, ' Well, I've measured myself with every man in the town, and Tm the tallest man in it,' and it might be quite true. But will even he be found qualified?

The trial day comes. Each is measured, from the man five feet six inches, to the very tallest. Suppose he is live feet eleven inches and three-quarters. The sergeant cannot let him pass. He is short. He must take his place among the very shortest as to getting into the Life Guards. He is the tallest man in the town, but he is short of the standard, and ' there is no difference' from the very shortest as to his exclusion from the Life Guards. 'There is a difference' in height, but not in qualification.

Thus it is with every sinner. He may be good, or bad, in the sight of men, but 'there is no difference, for all have sinned and come short of the glory of God.' If any man could say, I have come up to God's standard, and this is true, then there would be a difference; but 'come short' is written on every man's brow, therefore there is no difference.

Whether was Adam or Eve the more to blame? This might afford material for a long discussion, and at the end, the heinousness of their crime would be to us a matter of opinion. I have no doubt there might be some shade of degree as to heinousness; but one thing is sure — if their offences were not equally heinous, they were equally driven out. The cherubim that turned every way with the flaming sword, separated both equally from the tree of life; there was *no difference*.

When the rain began to fall and the waters to rise, after Noah had entered the ark, the people who had their houses high up might have been pitying the poor people who built low down in the valley, as they heard the screams of the drowning. By and by the water sweeps above the little hills, and then those on the high hills, in turn, congratulate themselves upon their high-built villas. But the water still rises; it enters their ground-floors; they rush out of their grand mansions or hovels — for there was no difference — and flee to the tops of the very highest mountains; but only find respite for a few moments, for ' all the high hills, under the whole heaven, were covered; fifteen cubits upward did the waters prevail, and the mountains were covered, and all flesh died that moved upon the earth .... and every man; all in whose nostrils was the breath of life, of all that was in the dry land, died, and every living substance was destroyed which was upon the face of the ground.' Under that judgment-flood there was *no difference*. Look across the wide, level sea, and consider the thousands of caves and stupendous mountain chains that it hides, the plains and valleys, the dens of seaweed and the fortresses of rock; and the level sea rolls equally over all, and there is *no difference*. Drunkard and respectable lady, the hoary-haired sinner and the infant at the mother's breast — all were under that fearful flood, for there was *no difference*. If you had been there, do you think you would have been made an exception of? You may be able just now to get anything that money can buy. Could money have saved you then? Prince and beggar, strong men and weak, bad and good, were all equally swept away. There was *no difference*. It has happened already, you see, and it will happen again — not with water, but with fire.

When Jehovah rained upon Sodom and upon Gomorrah brimstone and fire from Jehovah out of heaven,' there was *no difference*. All were equally destroyed: very bad and very good shared the same fate. This fearful, unprecedented shower falling out of heaven — brimstone and fire —took everyone by surprise, and destroyed every dweller there. ' He overthrew those cities and all the plain, and all the inhabitants of the cities.' There was *no difference*.

When Israel was sheltered in the house of bondage from the destroying angel's hand, ' it came to pass that at midnight Jehovah smote all the firstborn in the land of Egypt, from the first-born of Pharaoh that sat on his throne, unto the first-born of the captive that was in the dungeon.' Judge and prisoner alike found themselves face to face with death. In the palace and in the hovel the voice of mourning was heard; not one of all the doomed first-born escaped. These first-born might have been beautiful, amiable, educated, and accomplished, or they might have been vile, degraded, ignorant, and hardened; but there was *no difference*. It is with this God you and I have to do.

When Jericho's walls fell flat before the appointment, the ordinance of God, in righteous judgment 'they (the Israelites) utterly destroyed *all* that was in the city, both man and woman, young and old.' The strong man and the feeble woman, the active young man and the decrepit old, were equally slain by the edge of the sword. There was *no difference*.

The flaming sword of the cherubim, the flood of waters, the deluge of fire, the angel of death, and Joshua's sword, all preach to you and me with calm, decided voice, *'There is no difference.'* These things were written for us, that we might know what we may expect so that we might not leap in the dark. Nothing will happen which has not been told us.

A brother in the Lord could never get a young lady to think about eternity until he quoted this text, 'The wicked shall be turned into hell, and all the nations that *forget* God.' That word, *'forget'* seemed to haunt her. May it haunt you, dear reader I You do not require to deny God's existence, to mock at Him, to despise Him, to reject Him, to neglect Him; all you have to do is to forget God. Do you know the God who says, *'There is no difference'*? Have you forgotten that he identifies you with all descended from Adam? Have you forgotten the God driving our parents out of Eden, and placing a sword crying for blood? Our brother Cain soon forgot; our brother Abel remembered. Have you forgotten the God who swept away all in the days of Noah? Have you forgotten that He is the Judge of quick and dead, and as there was *no difference*, so there is a day coming when there will be no difference. In the judgment of the quick, ' all the goats are equally' on the left hand —'*there is no difference*.' In the judgment of the dead, ' the dead, *small* and *great* stand before God' — small and great sinners, young and old, king and serf, peer and peasant —' and *whoever* was not found written in the book of life was cast into the lake of fire,' for 'there is no difference' Your name may have been written on the communion-roll o{ any or all the churches, or it may have been written in the sheets of the Newgate conviction-book for murderers, but *'there is no difference.'* The lake of fire levels all distinctions. There may be, there are, many and few stripes; there may be, there are, great and small cups full of wrath, but every cup, be ft great or small, is *full*. The lake of fire — fearful thought — rolls its hideous sea of wrath and torment in one surging wave over all that have not been enrolled in the one book of life. In hell, and perhaps only there for the first time, you will believe that ' there is *no difference.'* Every one believes it there.

Let me ask you to look at another picture. Three men are hung on three crosses. If you look at them, you will see that 'there is *no difference*. If you listen to what they are saying, you will hear one at the one side mocking Him in the centre; and the one on the other side saying, 'Dost not thou fear God, seeing thou art in the same condemnation.' And we indeed *justly*, but this man hath done *nothing amiss.'* The one in the centre is saying, 'Father, forgive them, for they know not what they do.' Those suffering 'justly,' and He that did 'nothing amiss,' equally suffer, for 'there is *no difference*!' Those needing forgiveness, and He praying for their forgiveness, are under the same doom, for ' there is *no difference.'* Who are they? Those on either hand are two malefactors, or thieves, who die by the condemnation of their law. He in the centre was proved innocent, and He is the Judge of quick and dead. He has taken of his own free-will the load of sin upon Him, and, under sin. He cannot be cleared. Spotless, pure, holy though He was, He cannot escape. God can by no means clear the guilty. ' He hath made Him sin for us, who knew no sin.' He is under our guilt, and 'there is *no difference'* between Him and the thief— He must suffer. Dear reader, does not this explain all difficulty about an innocent, amiable, virtuous, accomplished lady being on the same level before God as a drunkard and a murderer? Here is God's perfect Son — yea, the very God-man — on the same level with malefactors, not for Himself, but for us. God became man, and gave Himself for our sins. This satisfaction that the innocent made for the guilty is offered to you, and you may freely have it, for 'there is *no difference.'*

If the eye of the vilest sinner in this world should perchance rest on this—an outcast from all society, one who has lost all friends and all self-respect, the tottering drunkard coming out of his delirium tremens — I tell you as from God, this Christ is offered to you as God's love-gift. You may reckon Him yours, and proceed upon it as if He were yours as truly as I or any other person in this world do so. You have as much right to claim Him as we, for *'there is no difference'* in God's sight —

'His blood can make the foulest clean,
His blood avails for me.'

Thus, my friend, for whom especially I write this, you have to take the lost sinner's place, for God says, *'there is no difference.'* As I have said before, I could know this only from God's Word. You have been as happy as a bird all your life, but you forget to find out what God thinks about you. I have tried to show you this from the Bible. I do not ask you if you feel it, for I am sure you never could, neither could any one feel all the catalogue of sins in Romans i. and iii. true against him individually; but God knows us better than we know ourselves, and this is His estimate of us.

From the same word, and therefore on the same authority, and on none other, I tell you that God has given you Christ. ' For God so loved the world that He gave His only-begotten Son.' I do not say that you are to feel that Christ is yours, any more than I asked you to feel all the indictment true against you. You are to believe that Christ is yours, as you believe the black accusation against you is yours, only on the authority of God.

I once asked a woman, 'Do you feel that you are condemned?'

'Yes.' she said.

'Now,' I answered, 'that is absurd. You may know and feel you are guilty, but you can only *believe* you are condemned, because you know you are condemned on the authority of the judge who has pronounced the sentence.'

So on God's authority, and on it alone, I know I am 'condemned already.' And on the same authority alone I know that 'Christ is for **me**,' me individually. Just because I accept God's estimate of myself, I have a right to accept God's estimate of His Son for me. I believe the record that God gave of His Son to lost sinners. It looks very humble to say I am too great a sinner, or something similar, thus comparing myself with other sinners; but the *humbling* bit is that '*there is no difference.*'

All are 'condemned already,' but only those who believe it reap the advantage of this. Advantage! What advantage can there be in knowing I am condemned already? Much, because only they who believe themselves condemned can claim a Saviour. And now the 'righteousness of God is by faith of Jesus Christ unto *all*,' that is to say, it is offered, in the person of Christ, equally unto every person in this world, but is only ' upon all them that believe; for there is no difference, for all have sinned.' 'All,' in Rom. iii. 9, are said to be ' *under* sin.' So, in ver. 22, all believing ones arc under righteousness. It is '*upon* all them that believe.' Righteousness is altogether and for ever outside of every man's attainment, for it must be perfect, and all have sinned. Read Rom. iii. 19 to 26. ' Where sin abounded grace did much more abound.' God has proved us all equally by nature and practice '*under sin*;' He now has placed all of us who believe '*under* grace.'

Thanks be unto God, my dear friend, though you began this paper not knowing yourself as God knows you, you may now, on God's authority, where you are, without moving, claim Christ 'the righteousness of God' as yours, and may rise to tell others like yourself what God thinks of us and what God has provided for us. It is in love that Me will not let you alone. If we are to be ' before Him ' for ever, we must be ' holy and without blame in love;' and if so, it is only 'in His Son' that this can be.

Virtuous or vile, decent or indecent, rich or poor, receive and rest upon God's Christ *now* as He is so freely offered you, and then you may believe (not feel) that your sins are in the depths of the sea, that the shoreless ocean of the love of God flowing through a crucified Saviour has rolled over your millions of sins, and you can triumphantly say, as you look at that ocean covering all that is against you, ' there is no difference.'

17

If any one is to be kept out of heaven for the believer's sins, that must be Christ, as ' He bore our sins.' God laid on Him our iniquities.

Clad in the skins of God's own making (type of the righteousness of God), Adam and Eve were equally clothed, there was *no difference*.

Shut in by God's hand into the ark of gopher wood, 'Noah only remained alive, and they that were with him in the ark;' but they all, great and small, man and beast, bird and creeping thing, lion and worm, were equally saved floating nearer and nearer heaven the higher the judgment waters rolled, for there was *no difference*.

Under Shelter of the sprinkled blood every house of Israel was safe even in Egypt, and all equally rejoiced around the roasted lamb, for there was *no difference*.

Under protection of the scarlet line all found in Rahab's house were equally safe when all in Jericho were destroyed, for there was *no difference*.

None of all those enrolled in the Lamb's book of life can be cast into the lake of fire. They shall never see the second death, for in that book there is *no difference*; once there, perfectly safe for ever. God's salvation to lost sinners must always be through judgment. We must accept His ordinance. What was there in skins of beasts, an ark of gopher wood, a few drops of blood, a red cord, or in a certain book? They are God's ordinance, God's perfect: way. It will matter little what we think will condemn or save, let us accept God's thoughts for both. God has written out our character. Read Rom. i. 29, ' Being filled with all unrighteousness, fornication, wickedness, covetousness, maliciousness; full of envy, murder, debate, deceit, malignity. Whisperers, backbiters, haters of God, despiteful, proud, boasters, inventors of evil things, disobedient to parents, without understanding, covenant-breakers, without natural affliction, implacable, unmerciful.' Gal. v. 19, 'Adultery, fornication, uncleanness, lasciviousness, idolatry, witchcraft. Hatred, variance, emulations, wrath, strife, seditions, heresies, envyings, murders, drunkenness, revellings, and such like.'

But I hear some one say, —

'That is the character of a heathen.'

'Yea, friend, it is thine — these are what thy heart is made of They may be kept under, but they are all there in germ, though not necessarily developed into transgression.'

'Nay, all these are not in my heart.'

'Well, I'm sorry to hear it.' 'Why?'

'Because only this character will be received at Calvary. Only what God has written about us will be accepted by Him: but coming to Calvary with this in our hands, we shall hear his voice saying, "" I, even I am He that blotteth out thy transgressions for mine own sake, and will not remember thy sins," and all are gone for ever..'

Why does not every one believe that his heart is desperately wicked? Because it is deceitful above all things, and cannot bear to hear the truth when spoken about itself. Accept the character God has given to you, and accept the Saviour He has provided for you.

Thou just and holy God,
Before Thee who can stand?
Guilty, condemned, all waiting wrath
In judgment from Thy hand

One sin deserves a hell,
A death that ne'er shall die;
Our sins like sands on ocean's shores

In millions 'gainst us lie.

Thou God of truth and grace,
We praise Thee for Thy way
By which the guilty may draw near —
Their guilt all put away.

Thy Christ who bled and died,

Up to Thy Throne has gone;
Himself Thy love-gift we accept.
We rest on Him alone.

We praise Thee as Thy sons
Before our Father's face,
As o'er our every sin now rolls
The ocean of Thy grace.

Would You Like to be Saved?

Our Justification

'WOULD you like to be saved?' 'Indeed I would.'

'And would you like to be saved in God's way?'

'Oh! yes. But I can scarcely see how any poor sinner like me can know that here.'

'Well, I wish to place before you a sure road to heaven for the unholiest of us all, and shew you how, by simply believing God, we may know that we are saved.'

'I read my Bible, and I am sure I believe every word in it.'

'I know there are few who doubt there is a God, or the leading doctrines of the Bible. But, by the help of the Spirit of God, I would try to tell you some plain truths which you may not know, or things about which you may have wrong notions — truths about God's relation to you, yourself, personally and individually, and about your seeing, receiving, and taking for yourself God's salvation.'

'Do you know that God loves **you**?'

'Ah! yes,' you say, 'he loves us all.'

'Quite true.' But sit down and ask yourself again, 'Do I believe that God loves me?' To convince you of it. He says in His Bible, and one word is enough from Him — 'God so loved the world, and you are part of that world.

But now you say, ' If God so love me, He will be merciful to me a poor, struggling, failing sinner, if I do the best I can, and He will overlook my many sins.' Now, this is a point upon which you need to be set right. His name is love; but He is as just as He is merciful, as true as He is gracious, and thus ' can by no means clear the guilty.' He can overlook nothing. You know that Jesus Christ, God Himself manifest in the flesh, came into our position, our place, under our sin, and died a great many years ago. He had no sin of His own, but put away sin by the sacrifice of Himself. Now, God says that He so loved us that he gave us Jesus, and all that we have to do is to believe in Him. Of course you believe that He came and died; but did you ever believe that God gave Him to you? 'Ah!' you say, ' I wish I could feel that.' But God does not ask you to feel it. He states what He has given to you, and asks you to believe Him. 'God so loved the world that He gave His only begotten Son,' whether you believe it or not. When you accept God's gift you believe in Him.

Jesus Himself told us this when on earth; and surely He did not mean to deceive us. He was speaking about the bitten Israelites in the wilderness. They were all bitten, and a serpent of brass was put upon a pole, and every one that looked lived. This serpent was given to the Israelites whether they looked or not. Supposing that one Israelite had said, I wish I could feel that the serpent is for me, what would you have said? 'Certainly: are you bitten? ' That is all you need. Are you a guilty sinner? then you have a right to believe that Jesus is yours. This is the simplicity of the Gospel, which has stumbled many great men, and which seems so foolish to the wise of this world.

People, when they are ill, or begin to think they are to die, try to pray, leave off bad habits, and be good, and do the best they can. Yet, though all these are very proper things to do, they will never save anybody. Supposing these bitten Israelites, instead of looking, had begun to put on poultices, and get ointments, and dressings, and mixtures, to counteract the bites — well, that would have been very sensible, men would say; but God said, look; do as I tell you: — Look to that serpent on the pole. So God's gospel is, ' Believe on the Lord Jesus Christ and thou shalt be saved.'

But you may say,' I am no worse than my neighbours. If I am lost many will run a bad chance; there are many worse than I am, and I only hope in God's mercy.' Now, this is all a delusion. One sin will damn any man for ever. Sin brought God's Son from heaven to become man and die. It is true many are worse than you, and that they will have a bad chance. That is the very reason I write this for you and for all, because most people are going to hell just now and do not know it. I did not make the calculation. Jesus Christ, who cannot tell a lie, said that there were two roads, a wide and a narrow; that most people go in the wide one, and few go in the narrow one; that the wide one ended in endless misery, and the narrow one in endless happiness. You have only one chance, which is to believe God who says that one sin will send you to hell. You have committed at least one sin. Now accept Christ as your own and only Saviour.

But the great deceiver of the world, that is the devil, who tries to do all he can against God's truth, if he finds that you will not believe yourself to be worse than other people, or that still you have a chance, will take another and opposite course, for the devil's statements are like the time of a bad watch, either too fast or too slow. He tells you that either you are too bad, or not bad enough. Now Jesus Christ came to seek and to save the lost. A man who said of himself that he was the chief of sinners is in heaven long ago. The blackest, vilest, most debased, most debauched, polluted, filthy, unclean, hard-hearted, evil-tempered, lying, covetous, thieving, murderous, grey-haired sinner that ever tottered on this side of the grave, is reached by Him who hung between two thieves for sin. God says it: that is all. We cannot understand it. Only this, He chose to do it, and now He tells us. His voice, dear sinner, is still deeper than you, 'Come unto me.' A thief that had reviled Christ after the hand of death was on him is in Paradise, we know. Why not you? And why not be saved now.? If not now it maybe never.

I once met a poor woman in the south of England. I began to speak to her about heaven and Jesus. She did not understand me. I asked her if she had ever heard of Jesus; she said, no most lamentable in this Christian land, so called). I told her that up above those skies Jesus dwelt, and He had so loved us that He had descended from heaven and had become a man. There was a condemned criminal lying waiting execution not far from where we were, and everyone was speaking about him. I said to her, 'You have heard about the man that is to be hanged.'

'Ah yes.'

'Suppose, as he lay in the jail, a knock the night before the execution was heard at the door, and a gentleman walked in, sat down, and said,—

'"You have broken the laws."

'"Yes, yes," the convict would cry.

'"You have been condemned."

'"Yes, yes, justly too."

'"You are to be hanged."

'"Yes, to-morrow."

'"I am the Queen's son; I have come from Windsor at Her Majesty's desire, and this is what I am to do: I will take that prison-dress which you have on and sit in your place, and you will take my dress and sit in my place." The convict in astonishment exchanges dresses; he wonders if he is dreaming; the Prince sits down in the convict-dress, and the morning comes; the executioner walks in; he passes the convict; he takes the Prince dressed in the condemned man's dress; he leads him out; he is hanged by the neck till dead; and the man that was condemned walks out free through the opened prison doors.' The poor woman looked in astonishment at this picture of what Christ had done for the sinner—defective in many points, still it impressed on her the great truth of putting the good and innocent one in place of the bad and guilty man.

'Now,' I said, ' this is what the God that created you and me tells us of His Son in this book. Can you read? '

'No,' she said.

'You will believe what I read from God's Word, this book, the Bible, that God has written for us. " Christ hath once suffered for sins, the just for the unjust, that He might bring us to God." (i Pet. iii. 18.) "When we were yet without strength Christ died for the ungodly." "While we were yet sinners Christ died for us."' (Rom. v. 6-8.) She gazed in wonder— she knew she was a sinner. ' Will you believe God,' I continued, ' that He loved you and gave you His Son, the glorious Prince of princes, who once died but is now alive again?' She looked amazed, and trembling said,—

'May I?'

'Not only have I authority to tell you that you may, but God has commanded you to do it, and you will never please God half so much, although you toiled, and wept, and prayed for a million years, as by obeying His voice and taking His gift.'

This is the substance of our conversation, though by the lapse of time I may have forgotten some things and put in others. It seemed to be used by God; for the woman professed at once to believe on Jesus, and to believe God that in Him she had everlasting life. I saw her next evening, and she had a calm joy in her soul; she was longing to hear about that glorious Prince who had been sent to die the convict's death, to preach liberty to the captives, and the opening of the prison to the bound.' She resolved to begin to learn to read, so that she might know the truth for herself from the Word of God.

But you may say, 'I am not so bad as she. I can read. I know all about Jesus. *I have always believed.*' Yes, you have always believed about Jesus, but have you believed that *He is yours*? You have always believed that He is the Saviour of sinners; but have you believed that *He is yours*? If you have not, you are still condemned, still unsaved, and, in all affection, I would earnestly entreat you, before you read another line, to lay down this book, and take God at His word, never heeding what you feel, nor whatsoever your heart may say (it is a liar); but believe God that he so loved you (put in your name), that He gave Jesus to you (put in your name — that is faith). You see you have not believed always that Jesus is yours, as I have said, but would repeat again, you have not to feel He is yours. If you thus believe Him, then all your sin is for ever gone, as between you and God you are justified from all things, your sins are cast into the depths of the sea, you can never come into condemnation, you are as sure of heaven as if you were there, for God has said it. Certainly your wicked heart within you is not gone. I have often met with poor, distressed souls who were una- ble to make out how people could know they were saved, thinking that if they were saved they should never have any sin in them. God says, if people (that is, saved people) say they have no. sin they deceive themselves. All the difference lies in this, having sin in me, and sin ON me. I once tried to put the way to be saved before a lit- tle girl who was wishing to know about it, and I think it shewed her the gospel to the saving of her soul.

'How many people were crucified on Calvary?'

'Three,' she replied. 'Two thieves, and Jesus between.'

'Were both the thieves equally bad?'

'Yes, they suffered justly.'

'Did both die alike?'

'No.'

'What made the difference?'

'One believed on Jesus, the other did not.'

'Now what about sin with regard to these three? The one thief that did not look to Jesus, had he sin in him?'

'Yes.'

'Had he sin on him? '

'Yes.'

'And Jesus, had He sin in Him?'

She thought a little, but she answered rightly, 'No.' (He was holy, harmless, no speck ever defiled Him, He could touch lepers and still be clean.)

'Had He sin on Him?'

'Yes.'

'His own?' 'No.'

'The thief that looked to Jesus, had he sin in him after he looked?'

'Yes.'

'Had he sin on him?'

This Cross still divides the world. We are all sinners, as were both the thieves. On one side are saved sinners, on the other unsaved sinners. On the one side are those who believe God that Jesus is theirs; on the other, those who do not. On the one side are those who have sin in them, but no sin on them, because they have left it on the spotless Sin-bearer; on the other, those who have sin both in them and on them. And all the people in the world die as those two thieves did. None ever died, or ever will die, without sin in them. The name of every man when he dies will be *sinner*. The name of each man was *thief* to the very last breath; but one died a saved *thief*, the other died an unsaved *thief*. The one set of men die saved sinners, the other unsaved sinners. The one die with sin on them, sinking them down to an awful hell; the other die with no sin on them, and are for ever with the Lord.'

'Now, will you not be saved?'

'How *can* I? '

'Simply **look**.'

'But I have often tried to look, and I have often tried to bring before my mind a picture of Jesus hanging on the cross for me.'

'Now, this is not the way at all: a vision of Christ on the cross, or a dream, or a thought, is not what God gives. Suppose I was laid on my death-bed to-night, and, as I lay, the devil came to me, and told me that I was not saved; suppose I said to him, "Some time ago I had a vision of Christ hanging on the cross for me."

"Ah!" he would say, "that was a delusion I brought before your eyes to deceive you."

"Well, but I dreamt one night that Jesus came close to me, and said, ' Thou art mine.' "

"It was all a delusion."

"I had a thought one day: it just flashed across me all at once, that I was saved."

" Only a delusion." And I could not answer the accusing deceiver. But I will tell you what will put him to flight. I take my Bible and I say, " God says that He gave me Jesus."

"How do you know that Jesus is for you?"

"Because God **says** that He so loved the world that He gave His only begotten Son."

" But do you think that so great a sinner as you can be saved by simply believing Jesus is yours? "

" Yes; for God says 'He that believeth on the Son HATH everlasting life.' " And the devil could say nothing; for it is written, "They overcame him by the blood of the Lamb and the *word* of their testimony." You see I would never dare to bring before him what I felt or what ideas had crossed my mind, but simply and so *what* God says. This is *looking* — this is seeing Jesus in the *Word of God*:

'Will you not be washed in His blood, and be made for ever clean?'

'But how can I? What do you mean by His blood? I have often heard about it, and have often tried, while lying on my bed, to bring before ray eyes the sight of His blood flowing from His wounded hands and feet, and from His pierced' side.'

'Now this is another mistake: blood is a figure for *life taken*. Seeing the blood means believing God about the death of His Son, instead of your death. Being satisfied with Christ's death in the room of yours, this is being washed in the blood. You see no real blood, nor vision, nor picture of blood; but in that blessed Book of God you read, " He was wounded for our (faith says *my*) transgressions. He was bruised for our iniquities, the chastisement of our peace was upon Him, and with His stripes we are healed." Isa. liii. 5. This is seeing the blood.

'Will you not **come** to Jesus.'

'But how can I? I have read in the Bible that He said, "Come unto Me, all ye that labour and are heavy laden, and I will give you rest;" and I have often wished I had been on earth when He was here; I wish I had seen Him pass my door, I would have watched Him, and have run to Him and touched His garment. But He is in heaven and how can I come to Him?'

'Now God has most beautifully explained this; for we have not to go up to heaven (Rom. x. 6) to bring Him down, nor to go to the grave to bring Him up; but He is risen and gone to heaven, and He has left His Word, in which alone He can now be found. This Word may be in your hands and in your memory, that Word which the Holy Ghost has written, and is now urging you to believe, that God so loved you as to give you Jesus. He is asking you in that Word to believe that He is yours. This is "coming to Jesus." Now that He is in heaven, His Spirit and His Word,— His Word from His lips and His Spirit in, through, and with the Word are all that are left; and will these not satisfy.? Have you never thought that if you saw your name written in the heavens, or on the sea-shore, and you knew that it had been traced by God's finger, you would then believe that you were saved; but do you think God will make another and special revelation for you.? No, no, — you must just take salvation as all the rest of us poor sinners have taken it, by believing the one Book.'

'But have I not to wait God's time?'

'God has only one time — that is, to-day. I read of to-morrow in the Bible. Pharaoh wished the frogs taken from him, but to-morrow. Tomorrow is man's time. Now, to-day, is God's. If you came to a stream, would you sit down and say, I will wait till it flows past and when it is dry, then I will cross.? Men are not such fools. God is waiting on you. He is calling you. He is beseeching you; and this is his one request. Take my Son whom I have given. He cries to every accountable and rational soul in this world. Will you have Him.?'

'Oh, if I could feel a something in me telling me that Christ was mine, I would believe it.'

'Quite wrong again. It is believing something outside of you, trusting Him at God's right hand, and resting on His *sure eternal Word*,'

You will not throw this aside, will you, and say, I like it, or I do not like it? The poor sinner, saved by the grace of God, who writes to you cannot save you, nor can any man. Tell God what you are to do; tell God that He loves you; tell God that you trust Him; tell God that you believe Him; tell God that He has given you Jesus; tell God that you believe that also; tell God *that* He laid all your sins upon Jesus; tell God that you believe they were *on Him*, and therefore are not *on* you; tell God you have gone astray, but that you believe Him that your iniquity was laid on Jesus. Thank God for a *finished salvation in Christ*, Tell Him how well-pleased He is with Jesus instead of you; tell Him that you are

'*A poor sinner and nothing at all,*
But Jesus Christ is your all in all.'

May God Himself shew you, for His name's sake, His simple Gospel of *Christ for you*. A beloved brother said, when coming out of the darkness of self, 'It is the simplicity that stumbles me. It is too good news to be true.' Yes, if man were in it; but it

24

is not too good when we consider with what a God we have to do. You see ..God can overlook nothing. He can FORGIVE anything. He can by no means clear the guilty. He can take us out of the guilty Adam-standing, and put us into a new, a resurrection Christ-standing. He can save to the uttermost the blackest, vilest sinner that accepts (simply accepts) His gift, Jesus. Will you not receive Him? You may be in poverty, in nakedness, in misery, but God presents you with Jesus. He might have created a world for every one of us; but that would have been nothing compared with what He has given — Jesus. You may have a hard light here to make ends meet, but having Jesus it will be all the hell you will ever be in. You may have every comfort, and be altogether moral and good as far as man can judge, upright and religious, but without Jesus this will be all the heaven you will ever have. Religiousness, goodness, kindness, beneficence, uprightness, amiability, will not save you. Acceptance of God's gift alone will do so.

Now, what is it to be, ere we part, perhaps, never to converse again for ever— God's simple gospel for the meanest, poorest, weakest capacity, so that even a fool may embrace it; or man's ways, follies, pleasures, religion, world? Jesus is offered to all. Some will accept Him, and some will refuse. You make God a liar if you do not accept. You make yourself a liar, and God true, if you accept Him. Some may know all about Christ the gift of God presented to them, and yet not know Himself Tis eternal life to know Him.' By not receiving Him, they trample under foot the blood of the life-giving Prince. Others receive Him and thank God for Him and are saved.

May the blessed Spirit, the witnesser of Jesus, open the eyes of every reader to see Him, incline every fellow-sinner to believe God, and accept His gift.

Call your heart a liar and believe the record of the only living and true God.

Nothing, Lord, I bring before Thee,
Nothing that can meet Thy face;
But in Jesus I adore Thee,
For the riches of Thy Grace,
   Jesus came in love from heaven,
By the Father's love was given,
From that death He now has risen.
    Which He died for me.
    Jesus died for the sinner,
    Jesus died for the sinner,
    Jesus died for the sinner,
    Jesus died for me.

' Come to me,' Thy lips have spoken:
   As I am, O Lord, I come;
All Thy laws I oft have broken,
   From Thy side afar did roam.

Boundless love hast Thou been showing
   Settling every just demand;
Jesus as my own I'm knowing,

Thus obey Thy great command.

This the work that stands for ever,
   All my works are useless dross;
Jesus mine! yes, nought can sever
   Me from Him of Calvary's cross.

Precious blood of Him forsaken
   On that cross, in wrath, by God, '
Cleanses me; His life was taken,
   When made sin for me He stood.

'Look to me,' He said, who's risen,
   Jesus Christ my Saviour Lord;
Mortal eye can't enter heaven.
   But I see Thee in Thy Word.

Trust Him, claim Him, O believe Him,
   All was done thy trust to gain;
On him rest, and now receive Him,
   Add with Him for ever reign.

'Ye Must be Born Again!

Our Regeneration.

THOUGH you knew all the duties incumbent upon a royal Prince, this knowledge would not make you a royal Prince. You must be in a position before you can act under the laws of that position. This is the natural order admitted by all men in human things, but quite reversed when they begin to speculate on divine things. God's order is this — I make you sons: walk like sons. Man says, try to walk like sons, and after a shorter or longer time you will be made sons. But we must be brought out of the kingdom of darkness before we can take the first step in the kingdom of light. Before we can enter this kingdom we must have a nature capable of enjoying it. A nature can be implanted only by birth; therefore we must be born again. This subject is gone fully into in John iii.

Nicodemus, a ruler of the Jews, came to Jesus, and said to Him, 'We know,' &c. Jesus answered him by saying, 'Except a man BE BORN AGAIN,' &c.

There is a great difference 'between what we *know* and what we *are*; a great difference between our attainments, education, talents, knowledge, and our standing before God, and our relation to God. Nicodemus was an inquiring man, who had been convinced of Christ's claims by external evidences, and whose conscience was now seeking after something deeper and more satisfactory. He comes with this profession of knowledge, 'Rabbi,' we know that thou art a teacher come from God: for no man can do these miracles that thou doest, except God be with him.' (John iii. 2.) Jesus, because He knew all men, and all the thoughts of men, answered not the words but the need of Nicodemus, by shewing that all his knowledge would never save him or any other man; for ' Except a man be born again, he cannot see the kingdom of God.' Nicodemus by nature, however well-in-structed, could never see God's kingdom.

I.— Christ Not a Teacher of The Old Nature. He Is First A Saviour, Then A Teacher.

In the present day, in certain quarters, we hear a good deal about Christ as the perfect man, the perfect example, and the perfect teacher; but here is the answer of Jesus Himself to all such compliments. He came not to teach the old nature — not to teach man as sprung from Adam, but to seek and save the lost, to give the new nature, and to teach saved men. The policy of all who have openly, or in thought, denied the divinity of Christ, is to laud His moral teaching and his Godlike example. They bring well known and fondly-cherished truths forward, as if only they believed and preached these great facts; but at the outset they forget this insurmountable barrier to all moral reclamation of the old nature of man, 'Except a man be *born again'* he cannot see the kingdom of God;

26

We find others, however, who know Christ not merely as a teacher, but who also believe in His divinity, that lie is God as well as man. In fact, many in our land know every fundamental doctrine in the Bible; but a mere knowledge of doctrine, however true, never introduced a son of Adam into the kingdom of God. Men may have learned what justification, and sanctification, and adoption are; they may be able to distinguish minutely between all the creeds, isms, and heresies, they may be theoretically orthodox, may be able to judge preachers and sermons, may be very ready freely to criticise most men they hear, and graciously pay beautiful compliments to their special favourites, as Nicodemus did to Jesus. They may know, moreover, about the new birth, its necessity and divine origin; but notwithstanding all this, they could not dare to say, as before God, ' Whereas we were blind, now we see.' The greatest amount of theological education never yet saved a man. Greed, or the belief in a certain amount of doctrine, has made Christendom, but never made a Christian. 'Ye must be born again.'

Others again, when their consciences have been reached, try to get this new birth brought about, and begin most zealously to train and trim, to educate and reform their old nature, quite ignorant of what is meant by 'born again.'

II. The Old Nature Unchanged and Unchangeable

Nicodemus wondered how a man when old could be brought again into this world; but if it were possible, what better would he be? He might have changed his circumstances by this new birth according to the flesh; but would he have changed kingdoms? He would still be in the kingdom of the first Adam; he would still be flesh; for Jesus goes on to say, 'That which is born of the flesh is flesh,' (ver. 6). Water never rose above its level: that which is produced is of the same nature as that which produces. We find people to-day who think that if they were in other circumstances they would have a better chance of getting saved. The rich man thinks that if he were poor, he might have time to think of religion. The poor man, if he could get ends to meet, and had a little more money, would have more leisure to think of God. But the difficulty is not so much in what is around us, as in what is *within* us.

Again, the aids of religion are called in, in order that *the flesh* may be *improved*; but after all attempts it is found to be only religious flesh. Man may have all varieties of it; but it never rose to see the kingdom of God. In nature, we speak of the animal kingdom and the vegetable kingdom. If we took a rose from the latter of these kingdoms, and cultivated it and trained it, and by our various arts made it produce all its varieties, we never by these means could bring it into the other kingdom — into the animal kingdom. Or, again, if I take a nettle from the roadside, and bring it into my garden or my hothouse, watch over, dress, water, and warm it, I may produce beautiful nettles, and beautiful varieties of nettle, but I never could get apples from it; that which is produced from the nettle is nettle. We can never gather grapes of thorns, nor figs of thistles.

Man by nature is in the kingdom of the first Adam: no amount of reformation, amelioration, cultivation, civilization, or religiousness, car bring one single man into the kingdom of God. Look through Great Britain and Ireland,—what is the object of the great bulk of the religious machinery.? Is it not for cultivating the flesh, in order that, after death, it may see the kingdom of God? This is no guess. It is the sad confession of godly men in all the churches—godly bishops, godly rectors, godly pastors, elders and deacons. All unite in the same complaint, and do their best against it. The majority of respectable religious people, as good as Nicodemus, a master in Israel, do not know the practical power of this truth which stands at the door of God's kingdom. They put salvation at the end of a long series of self-improving processes— God puts the salvation of the soul at the very beginning, and all duties that in their discharge can honor Him, are founded upon this fact. Man's chief end is (not to get the soul saved, but) 'to glorify God and to enjoy Him for ever'—starting with being saved for nothing as the means to this end.

III. The Absolute Necessity of a New Nature

Before I can enter God's kingdom I must have a new nature, that can appreciate, see, live in, and enjoy that kingdom. Ask a blind man what red is. He has no idea of it because he cannot see, because he has not the capacity. Educate him in the mixing of colours. Tell him that the blue and yellow mixed make green; he may soon remember this, and *know* much more; by that knowledge he never *saw* a colour.

The questions therefore of most importance to you are not, do you know doctrine? do you know Christ's teaching? do you know your Bible? do you know the evidences of Christianity? do you know that Christ is God, that Christ is a Saviour? that He is able and willing to save? You may know all that, and be lost for ever. But, are you born again? Are you a partaker of a new nature, a divine nature? Are you an heir of God? Is your standing now in Christ or in Adam?

Before I can see the kingdom of God, I must have the nature implanted that belongs to that kingdom. This is something more than a mere thought of sin forgiven, or righteousness obtained. It is a question of capacity, of fitness to enjoy, of likeness of nature. What an awful thought that so many religiously educated people are lost! What a hell, where the good, decent religious sons of Adam have to be for ever shut up with the profane and the drunkard, and the abominable and the unclean!

Reader, I entreat of you, think. Think for a moment, did Jesus speak truth or tell lies? If He spoke truth, those who have not *been born again*, however intelligent, educated, moral, benevolent, or religious, can never see the kingdom of God, and must, therefore, be swept away for ever with the lost, for there are only two places. What a hell! Frequenters of cathedrals and frequenters of gin-palaces, tract-distributors and pick-pockets, drawing-room-meeting religionists and the offscourings of the streets! Priests who, with solemn mien, pretended to stand between the people and God, and murderers who have been hung for their crimes! Teachers who knew everything in theology, and the profane, the swearer, the blasphemer, the infidel! These things will turn out true, whether you believe them or not. It was seen in the days of Noah. Is it to be your bitter experience? Hell is real. Eternal punishment is real. Christ's words are true, although they may be doubted, or denied by the majority of men. The awful fact remains. Stop, therefore, high or low, rich or poor, educated or uneducated, intelligent or ignorant, religious man or blasphemer, respectable or profane, think and ask yourself these questions. *Am I born again? Have I a new life?* — a life communicated by the Spirit of God through the truth — born not of flesh, but of water (the word, Eph. v. 26) and the Spirit. *Have I been born twice* — once into this world of Adam, and again into that of God? Friend, if you have not this new birth, it were better that you had never been born; but now as you are, and where you are, whenever you are convinced of the necessity of this new birth, look and live; believe and be saved; take God at His word: He says, 'Ye must be born again;' and in the same chapter it is written, 'As Moses lifted up the serpent in the wilderness, even so mast the Son of Man be lifted up, that whosoever BELIEVETH on Him should not perish, but have ETERNAL LIFE.' — What God demands, God provides.

IV. How the New Nature Is Implanted.

This new nature is not implanted by a process, but received by an act of faith. This new nature never sets aside as to actual fact the old, never amalgamates, never becomes incorporated with it, never improves it, but 'lusts' against it in the believer, wars against it, is 'contrary' to it. And how is it implanted? Reader, this is of the greatest importance to you. Are you to look for-the new birth in your own frames or feelings, to an ordinance or an act of man. A mistake here is fatal —' Ye must be born again.'— How?

Jesus answers this, and gives us the three things that are divinely and absolutely essential for the new birth (John iii. 7), seeing the kingdom (ver. 3), entering the kingdom (ver. 5), or having eternal life (ver. 15), all these being but different aspects of the same truth. These three essentials are —

1. Water (ver. 5).
2. The Spirit (ver. 5 and 8).
3. The Son of man lifted up (ver. 14).

Let us consider each shortly: —

1. Water.

'Except a man be born of water and of the Spirit, he cannot enter the kingdom of God' (ver. 5).

It cannot in any way refer to baptism by water, the application of literal water to a man externally, as that would only wash his body and could not touch his inner man. Some would read the text, ' except a man be born of baptism,' and of course by this doctrine Old Testament saints could not be in the kingdom of God, as they were not baptized. Circumcision could not save a man. ' Neither is that circumcision which is outward in the flesh... Circumcision is that of the heart in the spirit, and not in the letter.' (Rom. ii. 28, 29.) No change on a man externally can profit. He may apply much nitre and wash himself with much soap, but his leopard spots of sin still remain. Nor will mere education, reformation, cultivation, training of the old nature, turn flesh into spirit. ' That which is born of the flesh is flesh;' it may be decent or indecent flesh, religious or irreligious, pious or profane, but still flesh.

Some seeing this, and understanding it, have now asked what can the '*water*' mean. This has been answered in several ways. Some say it is the same as the Spirit; others that it is the same as the blood, but ' there are three that bear witness in earth, the Spirit, and the water, and the blood,' so that if water was only another way of expressing either the working of the Spirit oi the cleansing of the blood, there would be only two bearing testimony — the Spirit and the blood and the water standing for either. We can solve the question by asking what should have come into the mind of Nicodemus when Christ spoke of water? He, a master in Israel, knew of a laver where every priest had to wash before he could enter into the holy place, for no unwashed foot ever trod that holy place. He, a master in Israel, knew the book of Ezekiel, and the promise to be fulfilled in a coming day to Israel. ' Then will I sprinkle clean *water* upon you, and ye shall be clean: from all your filthiness and from all your idols will I cleanse you. A new heart also will I give you, and a new spirit will I put within you... And I will put my Spirit within you, and cause you to walk in My *statutes*; and ye shall keep My judgments and do *them*.' (Ezek. xxxvi. 25, 26, 27.)

A teacher in Israel should have been looking for the antitype of temple and laver, and the true water of purification sprinkled to cleanse from defilement. He should have been conversant with the 119th Psalm, which definitely explains what the water is (ver. 9): ' Wherewithal shall a young man *cleanse* his way? By taking heed according to Thy *word*.''

The water here spoken of by Christ and typified in the Old Testament, is the Word of God, the embodiment, the revelation of God's thoughts.

Let us search the Scriptures as to this: ' Being born again, not of corruptible seed, but of incorruptible, by the *Word of God*, which liveth and abideth for ever. For all flesh is as grass.' (i Pet. i. 23.) In our text 'flesh' is contrasted with the ' spirit,' here flesh is contrasted with the 'Word.' 'The seed is the Word of God' (Luke viii. 11). 'The righteousness which is of faith speaketh on this wise, . . . The Word is 7iigh thee ' (Rom. x. 6-8). ' Of his own will begat He us with the Word of truth' (James i. 18). 'Ye are *clean* through *the Word* I have spoken unto you' (John xv. 3).

These all show that the word is used by God in the new birth in that place where Christ speaks of water to Nicodemus, but we have more direct evidence in Eph. v. 26, 'That He might sanctify and cleanse it (the Church) with the washing of water by *the Word*.' Thus, from Old Testament type, from New Testament analogy, and from direct scriptural statement in both Old and New Testaments, the *water* in the new birth is proved to be the '*Word of God*.'

And most important it is to see this. How am I born again by *the word*? Water cleanses by displacement. Uncleanness and water cannot occupy the same space at the same moment: the water displaces the uncleanness, and thus cleanses. The Word of God does not act by teaching 'the flesh,' but by displacing all the thoughts of 'the flesh,' and putting in those of God.

The entrance of God's word gives light (Psalm cxix. 130). Man was lost by hearing Satan; he is saved by hearing God. Man, in his natural Adam-Standing, is a chaos — nothing in him can meet or please the eye of God — he is without form and void, darkness brooding over him. When God, therefore, begins to re-create him (for we are His workmanship, *created* in Christ Jesus unto good works,' Eph. ii. 10), He says, 'Let light be,' and light is; and it is by the entrance of His word that this is done.

This word of God judges everything in man; it puts God and His requirements before man. Human opinion is entirely set aside. By nature we are all apt to rest satisfied that there are many worse than we. If I am lost, many will have a bad chance, is sometimes said, and quite true, for God's Word tells us we are all guilty, and, as we saw in a former chapter, there is *no difference*,' all condemned already, equally condemned. We compare ourselves with one another, or according as men are estimated, bad, good, or indifferent. God's word comes like water, and washes out all our thoughts and opinions.

'It's my idea,' says one, 'If one tries to live a good life, this is all he can do.' Of course, this is your idea; but all our thoughts are evil, and unless God's Word displaces our ideas we are undone.

'It's my opinion,' says another, 'that we must just do the best we can, and trust in the mercy of God.' Of course this is your opinion—but the action of God's Word is like water to wash out our opinions. The first thing it tells me about myself and about all of us is that we are lost, depraved, guilty, condemned.

But more; the Word of God brings in God's mind about Himself instead of my own; it lets God think for me, God speak for me, God act for me; it makes me passive, because I can be nothing else.

'*Hear*, and your soul shall live' (Isa. lv. 3). Life is on its syllables—man begins to speak, to pray, &c., when he wants to be saved — God says, Hear! God is praying to us, and should we not answer God's prayer before we begin to pray? He does beseech men by us (2 Cor. v. 20). His prayer is easily answered. He says, 'Will you have my Son?' and the answer is 'Yes' or 'No.' By thus hearing the Word of God, and understanding it (Matt. xiii. 23), we receive a new life from God in which God's thoughts reside, and in which they act. Let us now look at the Spirit's work in regeneration.

2. The Spirit.

We must be born of the Spirit —not the Spirit apart from the Word — not the Word apart from the Spirit—not two births — but the one divine new birth. We see Spirit and Word as the *living water* (John vii. 38). 'He that believeth on me, as the Scripture hath said, out of his belly shall flow rivers of living water. But this spake He of the Spirit, which they that believe on Him should receive.' This was seen at Pentecost, when the rivers of living water (read Peter's sermon, a number of Old Testament quotations) flowed out to the salvation of thousands, the words of God carried home by the Spirit—hence living water; the Word is the water, but it is stagnant or dead without the Spirit—Spirit and Word make *living water*. Again, Jesus said (John vi. 6) 'the *words* that I speak unto you they are spirit and they are life.' Mere moral suasion, as it is called, never yet saved a man. This Word only operates as God's Spirit applies it. The vehicle is the Word, but the power is the Spirit.

If people are famishing in a town, and we intend to send supplies to them, we load the vans and waggons with bread and corn, and make up a large train. The entrance of these waggons will bring life to many a famished family, to many a dying man. Why delay, then? why is the train lying useless at this station where there is plenty? We are waiting for that powerful engine which will speed it along. Screw up the coupling, make all fast; and now not only is the feast ready, but feast and guests are brought together. Christ Himself is the bread, the Word is the waggon, and the Spirit is the engine or power that brings Christ in the Word to us poor perishing sinners.

God made a great feast, and bade many (Luke xiv. 16); none came, and 'none of those men which were bidden shall taste of my supper,' is now what God has said. No merely invited guest ever came. We preach 'Come;' we tell that all things are ready, that the feast is spread, the door open, that 'yet there is room;' but no man by this mere invitation ever came; as one has said, 'God has to fill the chairs, as well as the table.' Five yoke of oxen or a piece of ground are of much more value to a natural man than the richest feast of God. God has to provide the guests as well as the feast. If there were no Christ provided, there would be no feast; if there were no Spirit working, there would be no guests.

Ye must be born of the Spirit. Like produces like. 'That which is born of the flesh' is not merely like 'the flesh,' but is 'flesh.' and 'that which is born of the Spirit' is not like the Spirit, nor is it the Spirit (that would be incarnation), but 'is spirit,' and He dwells in that which He begets.

This is something quite different from 'the flesh' being pardoned, then taught, then toned down, pervaded, and sanctified by the Spirit. We have the man, the I, the existing person with undivided responsibility, *'born again'* by the thoughts of God acting in him in power, and the mind and nature of God communicated to him by the Spirit; and this now is the man's life, as the 'flesh' was his life before. No Christian can have his standing 'in the flesh.' Alas, that ever any of us should walk in the flesh: 'we are not in the flesh;' alas, the flesh is in us still.

A boat has been sailing on the salt ocean; it has come through many a storm, and, half full of the briny water, it is now sailing on the fresh water of the river. It is no longer in the salt water, but the salt water is in it. The Christian has got off the Adam-sea for ever. He is in the Christ-river for ever. Adam is still in him, which he is to mortify and to throw out, but he is not in Adam.

He has now a power, and a position, and inclination to judge himself. He knows himself. It was at this point that Paul exclaimed, 'I know that in me — that is, my flesh — dwelleth no good thing.' He is not two persons, but in the one person he has, and will have to his last hour here, two natures diametrically opposite, and actively opposing each other. He now sees that 'the flesh,' lusts against the 'Spirit,' but the Spirit also against the 'flesh,' in order that he may not walk as he used to walk; that these are contrary, and therefore never can be friends, and that he has in him, and will have in him, a foe that is neither to be trifled with nor trusted, but watched, warred with, and mortified.

But his life is in his new nature. He is now a 'partaker of the divine nature,' 'born of God,' 'an heir of God;' and thus it is with every one who is born of the Spirit, Jew or Gentile, for God acts here in sovereignty. Connection with Abraham only gave them a fleshly standing, but a new thing is needed by the Jew as well as the Gentile, and is as free to the Gentile as to the Jew.

The eighth verse of John iii. is a most blessed verse. In it we poor sinners of the Gentiles have got in. Reader, never quarrel with the royal prerogative of God's grace; read Rom. ix., and see that if we do not let God be absolute we have no chance of salvation, for we are all equally 'condemned already.' Praise His grace that hath now appeared to every nation under heaven.

But passing over Christ's testimony of the Father, as given in verses nine to thirteen— (prophets had prophesied, but here is *God himself*) —let us now look at

3. The Son of Man lifted up.

This, indeed, is our life. Christ said, 'Ye must be born again;' but here is another must that He mentions, 'As Moses lifted up the serpent in the wilderness, even so must the Son of man be lifted up: that whosoever believeth on Him should not perish but have everlasting life.' God says. Ye *must*, but He also says, I *must*. Your Adam-life is forfeited, and you are under condemnation. The Son of man lifted up is the answer to the forfeit. Satan, who has the power of death, and has every man in his power (for all have sinned), has been destroyed as to his power, his head having been bruised by Christ on the cross. (Heb. ii. 14.) But Christ is now risen, and can communicate His life to any one who believes in Him, He having satisfied every demand of God. The new birth is the communication of a new life. Christ beyond the doom of sin is that life; Christ incarnate before His death cannot be 'our life,' because the judgment against the old life can only be met in death.

The ' corn of wheat' *must* die before the fruit can be produced. The resurrection-life of Christ is therefore the new life preached to the *sinner*, and implanted in him on his *believing* —a life that is perfect, impeccable, indestructible, eternal as the Christ of God is — a life that has already [proved victorious over the cross of shame, over death's strongest power—a life that will ere long swallow up mortality.

The Spirit of God applies the Word that speaks about the lifted-up Christ whom we receive and rest upon for salvation, and this is the new birth. Such a life is offered only to a *sinner* —what a comfort! No righteous man, no earth-wise, no rich man ever entered the kingdom of God as such — only as justified sinners. None but *redeemed* sinners sing the song of that kingdom— none but those who, guilty, depraved, lost, have taken their place with roused consciences at the foot of the cross, and there seen the lifted-up Christ. All in that kingdom are *'new creatures'* clothed in 'the best robe,' with the 'ring,' and the ' shoes,' and ' the fatted calf slain. What perfection is in the Word of God I The Word tells me that unless I am born again I cannot enter God's kingdom; but the same word tells me that if I am born again (though only a babe now) I am as sure of spending eternity with my Lord as if I were with Him. No hatred of devils, no enmity of the world, no power of the flesh, shall keep me out. We enter God's kingdom by being born again. We *have* eternal life even now. We have the germs of heaven even here. We do not wait for that life; but Mie that believeth on the Son HATH everlasting life' (ver. 36).

We have tried to shew thus briefly what is meant by being ' born of water and of the Spirit' Read i John v. 6 —' This is He that came by water and blood, not by water only, but by water and blood, and it is the Spirit that beareth witness, because the Spirit is truth. For they that bear witness are three; the *Spirit,* and the *water,* and the blood, and the three agree in one.' (Correct translation.)

The *blood* is for expiation; that is, the Son of man lifted up on the cross, and His life taken for ours. ' This is He that came by water and blood' (1 John v. 6).

The water is for moral cleansing; that is, the Word of God applied in power to our consciences. Jesus ' came not by water only' (that is to say, not merely a teacher of the word), 'but by water and blood' (He came certainly as the great teacher, but also as the great sacrifice making atonement for sin).

The *Spirit* is the witness from the throne of God to the value of that blood in the presence of God, and the witness to our spirits by applying the word (water), and thus morally cleansing. He is also the source, the framer, and the power of expression of every new feeling, thought, affection, or purpose in the new creation, ' and it is the Spirit that beareth witness, because the Spirit is truth.'

These three agree in one, meet in one point, work out one thing in their testimony, and this is the testimony, that ' God hath given to us eternal life, and this life is in His Son. He that hath the Son, hath life' (i John v. ii, 12).

What any sinner, therefore, has to do in this new birth is to look to Christ on the cross; and where is he to look to Him now as crucified but in *the Word*. He is to believe what God says about His Son. God says I have given you

Christ (John iii. i6). I believe it: therefore I than): God. I do not ask myself do I feel it.? but God says it—I appropriate it as mine — I believe His Word by putting in my name where God puts His ' whosoever.' In this Word of God we get the Spirit's witness—that is, God's testimony about His Son. God does the *work:* we believe the *Word*.

Reader, are you *born again*? You are not satisfied with yourself Nor is God satisfied with you. You are not satisfied with your estimate of the work of Christ. Are you satisfied with God's estimate of it. 'The Spirit has come to tell out to us the value of that blood. Faith does not consist in my valuing it, but in my accepting God's value of it. God says, ' When I see the blood, I will pass over you.'

If you do not believe God's witness, the Spirit of God in the Word, about His Son, you simply make God a liar. Now you must either make yourself a liar or God. Do you nut think that it would be the better way to say, ' Let God be true and every man a liar'— myself the first liar.? A man does not like to be called a liar, but God says, ' every man.' Until a man calls himself a liar, he makes God one. ' He that believeth not God hath made him a liar, because he believeth not the record that God gave of his Son. And His is the record, that God hath given to us eternal life, and this life is in His Son.' As long as you look within yourself for one idea, one opinion, one thought, you are listening to a liar.

Call your heart a liar at once and simply take God at His word, receive His Son as He has given Him to you.

Reader, art *thou* born again? There was a moment that every Israelite had between being bitten and dying; that moment was given him to look and live. That is thy brief moment of life, hast thou looked and lived? God can do no more than He has done to provide life for thee. He spared not His Son!

Do not look to thy wounds, to thy sins, and think thus to get peace. Try no longer earth's prayers, or religions, or works of righteousness. They are but ointments to thy sores, that will never heal, but look away from all to the serpent on the pole. . The question is not, whether thou hast great faith or little faith. It did not depend upon the length of the look, nor the earnestness of the look, it was the fact of looking that cured the bitten Israelite. Look and live! thou hast only one brief yet sufficient moment of time.

But how are men spending this little moment. 'In making money, in indulging the lust of the flesh, the lust of the eye, and the pride of life! In gathering together the dust of their condemned cell into heaps and calling it richest In gathering the straws that lie in their prison, and making crowns, and, madman-like, playing at kings while death is written as their doom; and the door of escape stands still open!

God is standing over them with this awful word, '**Ye must be born again**,' and this other wondrous word, 'The Son of MAN must be LIFTED UP.' He delivered up His Son to death. What a holy God! What a just, righteous, truthful God! When sin was lying on the sinless Christ, He could not let it pass. Do you think He will let you pass now after that awful day at Calvary? It is there that we read the doom of sin. How shall we escape from Him if we neglect His 'so great salvation?' For it is not with God merely as a judge we have to do; for it was His love that planned and wrought the whole redemption work. Doubly bitter will be your cup of wrath that you have spurned the salvation of such a God who desires to be known by you as love; for in order that any poor sinner might be born again, '*God so loved the world that He gave His only-begotten Son, that whosoever believeth on Him should not perish, but have everlasting life.*'' (John iii. i6.)

Let us suppose that you are convinced of these important realities; that you are lost; that therefore your first need is a *Saviour*, not a *teacher*; that you have not a nature capable of enjoying God; that the new nature is gotten by your being born; born again of water (the word) and the Spirit, but you cannot understand how this comes about. You cannot understand what is meant by looking to Christ as the bitten Israelites looked to the serpent on the pole. Let me illustrate it by a conversation I had, one day, with a man who had been hearing the gospel preached, and with whom I had to walk some miles.

I began by asking, 'Have you ever thought of the great salvation?'

'Oh yes,' he replied; 'I have often thought about it.'

'And are you saved?'

'Well, I could not say that—I don't feel as I would like.'

'I quite believe that; but do you think any of us could ever feel perfectly right in this world? But are you at peace with God?'

'I never could say that I am satisfied with myself.'

'But, my friend, I did not ask if you were. It would be a very bad sign if you were satisfied with yourself. But are you at peace with God?'

'Well, I never could feel that I have peace.'

' But I don't ask if you feel at peace with yourself; I hope you never will. Have you peace with God?'

'To tell you the truth, I am not right.'

'How long is it since you began to think of these things?'

'About seven or eight years ago, in the north of Ireland, I was first awakened by a minister preaching on "*Ye must be born again.*" And often since that time I have been trying to feel God's Spirit working in me.'

'And you never have?'

'No; I could not be sure.'

'How could ever any one be sure of what was going on within him, especially as our enemy comes as an angel of light?'

'Well, what am I to do, then?'

'Jesus was the one, you remember, that said, "Ye must be born again." "Except a man be born of water and of the Spirit, he cannot enter the kingdom of God." Now, at the end of all this conversation, Nicodemus did not know h1ow to be saved, but only said, "How can these things be?" even when Jesus Himself was the great Teacher.'

'That's just where I am.'

'Now, what did Jesus do? He took him away to the picture-book for children, and showed him the picture of a dying man looking away from himself to a serpent on a pole, and thus obtaining life; and told him that 'as Moses lifted up the serpent in the wilderness, even so must the Son of man be lifted up, that whosoever believeth in Him should not perish, but have eternal life." Now all you have to do is to look and live.'

'But that is just what I've been trying to do, and what I don't know how to do: — what is it to look to Christ?'

'Now I can understand your difficulty; you cannot see Christ with the eyes of your body; you cannot see Him in vision; you say that you cannot feel His presence within you; you cannot feel that you have faith.'

'Exactly; what am I to do?'

'Allow me to give you an illustration.' In some such words I spoke with my friend, and gave him the substance of the following illustration, which seemed to clear away his difficulty; and I trust, by God's blessing, it may enable you to receive God's simple plan, and accept God's salvation for nothing.

You have a rent—say £10 a-year — to pay, having to maintain a large family, and having been recently in distress and out of work, you find it impossible to pay it. Let us suppose that I was able, knew your difficulty, took pity on you, and said to you,—

'John, I hear you have your rent coming on, and" having had very hard times, you will never be able to pay it. Now I wish you to use your money for your most pressing wants, to get food and clothing for your wife and family, and *look to me for the rent.*" You, knowing me, and hence believing me, would go away home with a burden off your mind and a happy heart. When you came home next Saturday with your wages, you would tell your wife to spend all the money in getting food and clothing.

'But, John,' she would Say, 'are we not to lay aside something for the rent?'

'Oh no,' you would answer; 'I met a man whom I know, and he said, *Look to me for the rent,* and I believe him.'

And thus weeks would go on, till shortly before the rent-day a neighbour comes in and says,—

'John, l have only got £5 gathered for my rent, and I don't know what I'm to do. How much have you?'

'None at all.'

'What I have you nothing gathered.'

'No, for a friend of mine said. *Look to me for the rent.*"

'And are you not getting anxious about it?'

'No.'

'Why?'

'Because I trust him.'

'Why?'

'Because I believe him.'

'Why?'

'Because I know him.'

By and by the rent-day comes, and even your wife begins to be suspicious and doubtful, but you have implicit trust in what I said — you have no difficulty in understanding what *look to me for the rent* means; and so, at the appointed hour, I walk in and make my word good, and am happy to find that, against all your neighbour's doubts, against all your wife's fears, and even against all your own tremblings, you have trusted my word and looked to me for the rent.

This is, of course, just an illustration, as I have no doubt you are at the present quite able and willing to pay your own rent; but in the matter of our salvation, though we might be willing, we are totally unable; so the Lord now says, 'Look to Me, and be ye saved.'

Christ on the cross has satisfied God's justice. He paid the debt for the sinner. Men are doing perfectly right things; praying, living moral lives, and giving money for charitable purposes; but all for the wrong end. All these will never save. God says, *'Look to Me for salvation,'* and then begin to use your time, talents, money, powers, for their legitimate end, to glorify God. Do not try to be holy in order to be saved. That would be like the man laying up for a rent which he could never pay. *'Look to me and be saved'* says God, and then be holy, because you are sure of salvation on the authority of God. Religion will never save you—even pure religion. God defines pure religion in James i. 27: 'Pure religion, and undefiled, before God and the Father is this, to visit the fatherless and widows in their affliction, and to keep himself unspotted from the world.' By the deeds of the law we cannot be justified; therefore by doing all this we cannot be saved. Religion is the life of a saved man, not the efforts of an unsaved man to get saved. We do not try to do good in order to get a new nature, but we try to do good because we have received a new nature. The work which God will accept from you is not to the cross, it *from* the cross to the crown. Jesus did all the *saving-work*. He brought the cross to our level. Get saved by looking to Him, and then live to God. Do not look to the feeling of being saved—look away from what is being wrought in you to what was wrought *for* you. We are not saved on account of the Spirit working in us, but by means of His work—we are saved on account of Christ dying for us. We are not saved by faith but *through* faith. ' Look to me and be ye saved, all the ends of the earth.'

Lie down as a wounded, helpless, ungodly sinner, and look away from yourself to Jesus crucified for sin.

Look unto Me and be ye saved — Look, men of nations all; Look rich and poor, look old and young — Look sinners great and small!	*Look unto Me and be ye saved —* Look from your doubts and fears; Look from your sins of crimson dye, Look from your prayers and tears!
Look unto Me and be ye saved — Look now, nor dare delay; Look as you are — lost, guilty, dead — Look while 'tis called to-day!	*Look unto Me and be ye saved —* Look to the work all done. Look to the pierced Son of Man, Look to your sin all gone!

Do you feel your Sins Forgiven?

Our Assurance.

Do you *feel* that your sins are all forgiven? 'Indeed I do not; but I *know* they are.'
'Now, I cannot understand that. How can any one know it?'
'If you had wronged me, and I told you that I forgave you, would you not know it?'
'Most certainly; but how can you say that God ever told you that He forgave you? Did you just feel at a certain time something that you thought was God's voice, inwardly telling you that your sins were pardoned?'
'I certainly did not.'
'Then how can it be? I have tried to get converted as hard as any man could; I have prayed for grace, for strength, for the pardon of my sins, and for the Holy Spirit, and I do not yet feel any difference, and I never could feel as I have heard some men say they have.'
'I quite understand you; I was for years in the same condition.'
'Then how did you get out of it? I know ah about the plan of salvation, about the work of Christ, and the necessity of the Spirit; that we must be justified by grace through faith alone without the works of the law; that the promises are all most certainly secure to them that are in Christ; but how am I ever to know whether I am in Him or not?'
'I know that you may have heard some Christians say they *feel* they are pardoned, they *feel* they are saved; but this only tends to mislead. It did mislead me, and I have no doubt it is misleading you. These Christians may mean a right thing, but they state it wrongly. I feel happy because I *know* that my sins are pardoned; and I will shew you how I know that by and by; but I do not *feel* that my sins are pardoned. Let us suppose a case. A poor widow has no money to pay her debts. The creditor comes demanding his righteous due. A friend steps in, and says to the creditor, "I'll pay you the widow's debt;" he puts down the money, and the creditor hands him a slip of paper on which is written, "Received from Widow Blank the sum due, settled," with the creditor's signature affixed. The receipt is handed to the widow, and she feels very happy *because* she knows that her debt is paid. If you were to call that day, and say to the widow, "Do you *feel* that your debt is paid? " what would she say?'
'Feel it! What do you mean? There is the receipted account. I don't feel that it's paid, but I *feel* very happy *because it is paid.*'
'Now, do you not see the difference? The feeling is all right, but I do not feel my sin pardoned. I know it, and hence feel happy.'
'But does it not say somewhere in Scripture that the Spirit beareth witness with our spirits?'
'Now, from the very fact that you speak so vaguely about "somewhere in Scripture," I fear that you do not know well what Scripture is. The Bible is not a number of texts strung together at random: it is a perfectly arranged whole. Truth in a wrong connexion is the worst kind of error. You find in Romans viii. 16, this most blessed

and wondrous revelation from God, that " The Spirit itself beareth witness with our spirits, that we are the children of God." Mark carefully, this is not given as a ground to know that our sins are forgiven; but comes after the whole revelation of the truth concerning what we have done and what we are, and how our responsibilities are met. It comes after the triumphant assertion of Romans V. I, " Being justified by faith we have peace with God," and that crowning triumph after every question has been settled against us, " There is no condemnation" (Rom. viii. i).   At peace with God, and no condemnation, we now advance into our peculiar place among the creatures of God. Angels are at peace with God and have no condemnation, but they are only servants. Here is something additional, "We are sons of God." Being taken from the swine-troughs, and getting food and raiment, we would therewith be content, glad that we were in the house at all, even among the servants. But higher than servants aie we become, even sons. We may well pause, and say, is this presumption? Dare I say that all things are mine? that I am a child, a son, an heir of God? Yes! indeed you may; the Spirit has been sent to dwell with you and to be in you, as coming from the throne revealing to your spirit (which can now discern spiritual things) that, without presumption, you may lay claim to the title, the relationship, of son of God, heir of God, and joint-heir with Christ. That Spirit is within every believer, and seals only saved ones. He quickens the unsaved. God has sent forth this testimony, and he that is a believer has the "testimony in himself" (i John v. 10). The important point I wish you to see is this, that the Holy Ghost is never said to bear witness to me, by any internal feeling, that I am at peace with God. It is after a man knows he is a saved man that then there is a step further shewn him — namely, that he is a son. He is not only out of prison: he is set at the table of the King, whom he calls "Abba," that is, Father.'

'I quite understand the distinction, but I never saw it before; but if I could know that I was at peace with God I would be quite satisfied.'

'Yes, but God would not; however, this is the first point for you to know—"being justified by *faith* we have peace with God," not by the *feeling* of faith.'

'But don't some people feel it while others do not.?'

'Not at all. What I am contending for is, that the forgiveness of sins is a thing that can be felt by no one: and, unless the knowledge of it is founded on the word of God, and that alone, for every one, individually, it will be sinking sand for a death-bed. Scores of anxious people have been deluded into the idea that they knew the gospel when some pleasing emotion passed through their minds. When Satan sees people awakened, and that he cannot keep them quiet, he takes his stand beside the preacher of the gospel, and while he is inviting them to the rock, Satan pushes out planks of feeling. A drowning man will catch at a straw, and the poor troubled one finds a little relief in resting on some plank of quietness of conscience, till storms rage, and then he finds himself with nothing beneath him. I am therefore suspicious when a person tells me he is "a little better." If he does not believe the gospel, he has no right to be any better, and if he has taken the good news to himself, he is entitled to be at perfect peace.'

'Then you don't allow of any feeling?'

'Most certainly I do: but what am I warranted to feel? If I could tell you that you were saved, and you believed it, would you not feel happy?'

'Of course I would.'

'This is what I feel — whenever I say to myself, "I'm saved," don't I feel happy? and the more I realise that my knowledge that I am saved depends only on God's word, the more happy I become.'

'Is there nothing about this "feeling saved" in the Bible?'

'Indeed, there is not. You can easily satisfy yourself by turning to a concordance. Never once is the word put beside "salvation," "forgiveness," or, in fact, anything about a man's peace with God, but we find, in Luke i. 77, that part of John's commission is declared to be " to give KNOWLEDGE of salvation," and in many parts of Scripture we find "knowing our sins forgiven," " knowing in whom we have believed," "knowing we have passed from death to life," "knowing we are born of God." Did Abraham feel he was to have a son when he was so old? No! but he knew it. And how did he know it? Because God said it. He felt glad because he knew it, because he believed what God said. It is really because people do not believe that God mean exactly what He says, that we see so many intelligent men who cannot say whether they are saved or not.'

'But I have often thought that I had received Christ and trusted in Him alone; but I find my faith so incapable of producing effects.'

'But did you start saying "I'm saved," before trying to do anything?'

'Oh no! I was always waiting for fruits.'

'Fruits of what? fruits of doubt? Suppose you had got the right fruits, would you then have believed you were saved?'

'Oh yes!'

'That is to say, you would trust the fruits you brought forth rather than God's word — not for your salvation, but for your knowledge of it. But you must be saved, and know you are saved, before one acceptable fruit can be brought forth — else the works are legal. All evangelical obedience is done by a man who is saved, and who does it because he knows that he is saved.'

'Then am I to do nothing?'

'Absolutely and literally nothing. You must take salvation exactly as the thief on the cross did. He could not turn over a new leaf; his last wretched leaf had been turned in reviling his Saviour. He could not do any work for God, for there was a nail through each hand; he could not run in the way of God's commandments, for there was a nail through his feet. And until you stand still and realise that there is a nail through all your self-righting activity, and a nail through all your carnal agility, and accept salvation for nothing, knowing that you are saved simply on the authority of the bare Word of God, you will never be saved. We do not look inward to what we feel, nor outward to what we do—but to the Son of man lifted up, and to God's account of how well He is pleased with Jesus.'

'Well, I think I see what you mean, and it clears up a real difficulty. I am not to examine to see if I *feel* better, *feel* saved, *feel* forgiven, or *feel* happy; but here is the next difficulty—how am I to know it?'

' I well remember that when I began trying to feel converted, I felt myself becoming worse and worse, and my heart getting further and further from peace. Then I began to study this and that theological question, I knew all about what Calvinism and Arminianism were — studied my Bible till I knew its contents pretty well, but at last I found I was not on the right track for salvation at all. I was thinking that salvation came *intellect-wise* and not *faith-wise*.'

'But a man cannot be saved apart from his understanding?'

'Most certainly not, no more than he can be saved against his will; but the eyes of his understanding must be enlightened, that he may be made willing to receive the gift of salvation in God's way. You see if God had made His salvation dependent upon education or intellect, lie would have left the great mass without the chance of salvation until they were tutored up to the requisite point; but as there is *one salvation* for high and low, rich and poor, educated and ignorant, so there is *one method* of receiving it, and of course that must be according to the standard of the most unlearned. Hence the truth of the remark that a friend made to me, " Intellect never helped me to Christ, but it often hindered me."

'I was trying to explain this (which I believe to be of the greatest importance) to some poor people, and I tried to illustrate it in this way. If, in travelling by rail, I had a first-class ticket, I could travel one part of the journey in a first-class carriage, another part in a second, and another in a third, and the railway officials could find no fault; but, if I had only a third-class ticket, I must remain in the third from beginning to end. Thus, in regard to salvation, the educated man can come-to the uneducated man's platform; the uneducated cannot rise to his: therefore it is on the common platform on which all men can stand that God treats concerning salvation.

'This is the great difficulty; this is why not many great, not many wise, and not many noble, can afford to come low enough among the common run of people, to take a guilty sinner's place, receive a lost sinner's Saviour, and rejoice in a condemned sinner's pardon. This is why Christ taught that men had to become like little children before they could get into the kingdom of heaven.'

'I see the justice of your remarks; but tell me, now, how am I to get into the Kingdom.'

'As you said before, you know that it is *of grace* — that is to say, God is waiting to give it to you *all for nothing,* without a feeling in payment, without a prayer as the condition of it, just as the widow's friend dealt with her debt. That it might be of grace, it was made to be by *faith*, not by *attainment* either in intellect or feeling. This is the impression that has been sometimes left upon my mind, after having heard the gospel stated — that faith is the condition which God has demanded from the sinner, in order that he may be saved — that the great Physician will heal the most wretched, sin-burdened soul, but he must receive faith as his *fee*. Now this, as you have no doubt found, would be the most difficult of all fees to procure. Feeling is hard to get up, but faith is harder. Faith is the mere apprehension of grace — thankfully accepting what God has already freely given. Faith puts God in the chief room as the giver, it being more blessed to give than to receive, and lets him do everything, man being the silent and passive receiver of blessing. Faith has to do, not with what I feel toward God, but what God feels toward me, what He has done for me, and what He has told me. Faith does not look into its own formation — it looks out to God's provided substitute for the sinner. Faith does not tell me to *feel* that I am converted, but it fixes me down to the Word of God. Faith tells me to take God at His word. Faith has not to do with what I am thinking of myself, bad or good, but it lets God think for me.

'Two things are to be distinguished, "salvation" and the " knowledge of salvation." First, How am I to get saved? and then. How am I to know it.?

'First, then, my *salvation* depends solely and entirely upon the work, the *person*, of Jesus Christ our Lord. (My salvation is supported by His work; His work is supported by His person.)

' Secondly, the *knowledge* that I am saved depends solely on the record, the *word*, the testimony of God. " He that believeth not God, hath made Him a liar, because he believeth not the record (testimony) that God gave of His Son." A man is saved on account of Christ having died in his place, the moment that he accepts Christ; he knows that he is saved whenever he believes the record that God gave of His Son.'

'Well now, tell me shortly what "believing in the Lord Jesus Christ is." Of course I believe He is able and willing to save anybody. His atonement is sufficient, and His offer free and full; but how is He to become mine.?'

'What is it to believe in a man.? What is it to believe in a bank? You do not believe in one who is in the blacklist—but you can look around and say to yourself, " Well, I believe in so and so," and it is just the same with Christ: I believe in Him—not merely in His historical existence — but I trust Him, I receive, I rest upon, Him alone for my salvation.'

'In a word, then, what should I do? I am wishing to take God's way, and willing now to do it. When I begin to go through trains of thought, I feel I get confused, and I should just like to know in a sentence what my path ought to be.'

'*Take the lost sinner's place, and claim the lost sinner's Saviour!*'

'Will the claim be allowed?'

'Yea, God commands thee to claim Him.'

'Can I claim Him?'

'Only a lost sinner can.'

'I am allowed, urged, besought, commanded to take Jesus as mine; surely I have nothing to lose—yea. Lord, I believe Thee, Jesus is mine.'

'I take comfort from the fact that my sins were laid on Christ—I do not *feel* they were there, but God says it — "He was wounded for *our* transgressions;" not for those of angels — they had none; not for those of *devils* — they can claim no Saviour; but for those who take the sinner's place—'The chastisement of *our* peace was *upon* Him." Therefore it would be unjust to lay it on me believing in Him. He is a real Saviour for real sinners. My only qualification for such a Saviour is that I am such a sinner. And now I believe my sins are not on me — not because I feel them gone, for I do not, but because God says they were laid on Christ.' (Isaiah liii. 6).

Robert M'Cheyne says, 'We must not close with Christ because we feel Him, but because God has said it, and we must take God's word even in the dark.' We do not *feel* we have faith. We accept God's way of dealing with sin.

Man would try to settle God's claims. God Himself has settled the claims, and offers the settled account for nothing. Man would try to make his peace with God. God has come and '*made peace*,' Christ Himself becoming '*our peace*," and now He '*preached peace*' for the acceptance of all (Eph. ii. 14-17). Most anxious inquirers seem to think that we have to fight against ourselves in order to be saved, whereas we fight against ourselves because we are saved. We have a race to run, but it is not *to* the cross, it is *from* the cross. Man's way is to believe because we feel: God's way is to feel because we believe, and believe because God has said it. Dr. Chalmers says, 'Yet come the enlargement when it will, it must, I admit, come after all through the channel of a simple credence giving to the *sayings of God*, accounted true and faithful sayings. And never does light and peace so fill my heart as when like a little child, I take up the lesson, that God hath laid on His own Son the iniquities of us all.'

Take the lost sinner's place, and claim the lost sinner's Saviour.

No *works of law* have we to boast —
By nature ruined, guilty, lost,
Condemned already; but Thy hand
Provided what Thou didst demand:
We take the guilty sinner's name,
The guilty sinner's Saviour claim,

We do not *feel* our sins are gone,
But *know* it from Thy word alone;
We know that Thou our sins didst lay
On Him who has put sin away:
We take the guilty sinner's name,
The guilty sinner's Saviour claim.

No *faith* we bring.   'Tis Christ alone —
'Tis what He is, what He has done.
He is for us as given by God,
It was for us He shed His blood:
We take the guilty sinner's name,
The guilty sinner's Saviour claim.

Because we *know* our sins forgiven,
We happy feel: our home is Heaven,
O help us now as sons, our God,
To tread the path that Jesus trod:
We take the guilty sinner's name,
The guilty sinner's Saviour claim.

The Work of the Holy Spirit

Our Comforter.

WE are not saved *on account* of the Holy Ghost's work in us; we are saved by *means* of it. We are saved on account of Christ's work for us. The more the Spirit works within us the more shall we desire that work to go on; but the work of Christ on Calvary is finished, and this is our resting-place, our peace, our security. We never can (or never ought) here below to get satisfied with the work of the Spirit wrought within us, but we are satisfied with the work of Christ done for us, and this is eternal rest, this is faith. Many sadly confuse these two divine works. Anxious inquirers are constantly looking within to see what is going on there, instead of looking outward to what was done on Calvary. I wish to draw the reader's attention to three most precious operations of the Spirit of God as seen in the beginning of John's Gospel,—

First, *Born of the Spirit*; chap. iii. 5-8.
Second, *Indwelt by the Spirit*; chap. iv. 14.
Third, *Communicating the Spirit*; chap. vii. 3.

I. Born of The Spirit.

Many think that regeneration, or the new birth or quickening, is a process that goes on subsequent to justification. This is a mistake. Regeneration neither goes before nor comes after justification, but is at the same time and is an instantaneous act performed by the Spirit of God, communicating the life of Christ to a man formerly dead in trespasses and sins and having nothing whatever in him that could be transformed into this new creation which He implants. There are two errors against which we must guard:

First, not recognising or acknowledging the Spirit's special work in regeneration; and

Second, confusing or mixing this with Christ's work done for us.

1st. *It is by a special act of absolute grace that -we are born again by the Spirit.* 'The wind bloweth where it listeth,' and so the Jewish Pharisee is compelled to allow God to act as a sovereign. What would be the use of Christ coming, living, dying for sin, rising beyond its doom, and His present intercession, unless the Holy Spirit were here applying to individuals that work, that life by the Word. It is not His influence merely, but Himself, who is now on earth. It is not His Word merely, blessed and essential as it is, but Himself, who applies that Word. Look at the feast in Luke xiv. If Christ had not come and died and risen, there would have been no feast to offer, but if the Holy Spirit were not here, none would come to the feast. So the parable tells us, 'Compel them to come in;' and the Holy Ghost is the great compeller, making them willing. This is His special work on individuals, not His general work in the world. His work on the world is not in the way of *mercy* but of *conviction.*

In John xvi. 8, we read, when He is come He will *reprove* (literally, *convict by proof to its confusion*) the world —

(i.) '*Of sin,*' because the great sin of which God holds man to be guilty is the crucifixion of His Son; and the presence of the Holy Ghost is the great proof of man's refusing Christ, for the rejected Christ has sent the Spirit, and His presence is continually crying, 'where is the brother?' hence it is said, ' of sin, because they believe not on Me.'

(2.) '*Of righteousness.*' If man is an ungrateful sinner, God is a righteous God, and if sinful man gave his Saviour a cross of shame, a righteous God gave His Son a throne of glory. This is the great act of righteousness between God and the man Christ. 'Sit thou at My right hand until I make thine enemies thy footstool.' Ps. ex. i. The presence of the Holy Ghost on the earth is the proof of the righteousness of God. Christ having perfectly glorified God, God glorifies Him as a matter of justice, crowns Him with glory and honour; and we see Him, not by the natural eye, for Christ is not yet manifested on His own throne, but in the interval between rejection and triumph, the Father in righteousness has set Him down on His throne, and sent down the Holy Ghost to testify that He is glorified; therefore it is said, 'of righteousness, because I go to my Father, and ye see me no more.'

(3.) '*Of judgment,*' because, since Satan could not hold Christ in death, a power stronger than Satan's must have appeared, whose power over death must therefore have been set aside and himself judged, for 'through death He destroyed Him that had the power of death, that is, the devil.' The Holy Ghost has come to tell us of this great act of judgment; because the very fact that he has come proves that Christ is risen and is in glory; and the fact that Christ has risen proves that Satan has been judged; and since Satan is ' the prince of this world,' the world has been judged, being set aside in its chosen head; therefore it is said, 'of judgment, because the prince of this world is judged.'

Such is the action of the Holy Ghost *on the world* to its confusion and shame: but His work in quickening is quite a distinct thing. He does not work on ' the old man' in me and make it better, and thus gradually save. He shews me that it cannot be mended. He shews me that I am 'guilty,' 'condemned already,' ' lost,' 'alienated,' 'evil only,' 'continually evil,' 'without God,' ' without hope,' 'without strength,' Mead.'

I have heard men speak of a remaining spark in the bosom of the unregenerate that required merely to be fanned into a flame by the influences of the Holy Ghost. This is unscriptural (read Gen. vi. 5, &c.). I have heard such speak of a seed of good in every man which the Holy Ghost cultivates, and this they call the new birth. This is utter confusion, and an entire misconception of the figure. Man's co-operation in regeneration is not required, because he has no power to cooperate. He is dead. ' That which is born of the Spirit is spirit.' The work is altogether of God. As it was God who in His own heart before the foundation of the world, planned redemption, and as it was God in His Son who, eighteen hundred years ago, before we were born, secured our redemption, so it is God by His Spirit who now, without our endeavour, apart from our effort, applies this redemption. In fact, the first thing God does is *to make us willing.* How entirely is this work of God! He was alone in eternity; He was alone in creation; He was alone in redemption; He is alone in regeneration which is merely redemption applied. God does not *find* us children; He *makes* us children. But we must look now at another error.

2d. *Confounding the work of the Spirit in us with Christ's work for us.* While the Spirit of God is the sole agent, the truth of God is the sole instrument which He employs. We cannot see the Spirit; we can see the Word. We cannot see His operations: we can read His record about Christ. No doubt it will be merely letters without meaning, until He opens the eyes; but He works only in His appointed channel. He never tells us to look inward even to His own operations, for peace, but *outward to Christ.* That is the most Spirit-honouring preaching of the gospel in which you hear most of Christ. Once I heard a very earnest man preaching to anxious inquirers, and he was dwelling continuously and exclusively upon the Spirit's work — its signs and characteristics — with the effect of confusing many of his hearers. For who could obtain scriptural peace with God from what he felt? We get a healthful and heaven-born conflict by marking the Holy Ghost's operations within us, but never peace. This we get by gazing at the Lamb of God on Calvary. I thought, as I heard the preacher, ' I wonder if the Holy Ghost would preach in that way if He were standing there,' and 1 immediately remembered, that ' He shall not speak of (from) Himself,' ' He shall testify of Me;' that is. He will preach Christ. ' He shall take of mine and shall shew it unto you.' ' He shall glorify Me.' This is spiritual preaching, because the preaching of the things of the Spirit, and as He Himself preaches. I believe the more we are depending on the Spirit's working, the more we shall preach what the Spirit wishes us to preach about, and look to Him to apply it. When we begin to point the anxious inquirer to the Spirit's work, this is not how the Spirit Himself would deal with him.

If I began to speak to a working man sitting down to his dinner, and said to him, ' Do you know the muscles employed in mastication?'

'What's that?' he would likely say.

'Well, in eating.'

45

'Indeed, I do not."

'And you do not know the nerves that supply them?'

'I'm sure I do not.'

'And the beautiful mechanism and arrangement by which the food is converted into a bolus, and introduced into the stomach?'

'Now you are surely laughing at me.'

'Oh no, I'm not, but all that is most true and interesting; but tell me what do you know?'

'Well, sir, I know that I am hungry, and that this is a good dinner.'

This would be the common-sense and appropriate answer. Even the physiologist, when he is hungry, does not think much of how he eats. The two great points are, that he is hungry, and that he has a good dinner. Some are hungry and have not the good food, others have the food and are not hungry. But the qualification for enjoying food is not a knowledge of *how* to eat, but the being hungry. We do not need to know how we are born again in order to be saved. We do not need to know all or anything about the Spirit's work within us in order to get peace (there were people, in Acts xix. 2, who were believers, and who yet said, ' We have not so much as hoard whether there be any Holy Ghost'), but we must know about Christ's work for us before we can be saved. The greatest physiologist might die of hunger. We might know everything about the Spirit's work, and yet be lost for ever, because we had not received and rested upon Christ offered to us in the gospel.

We are justified by *faith*, but the experience of what goes on within me is sensation, and not *faith*.

Some men seem to have a difficulty with anxious souls (believing them to be dead), to know what to advise them to do. It is the Spirit that quickeneth. Some, therefore, tell sinners at once to pray for the Spirit, thinking thus to simplify matters by reducing it to common-sense — as it seems very plain, since the Spirit quickens, noticing is easier than to cry for that Spirit. But it is not so easy, for a dead man cannot cry. Some, again, tell them to believe the record God gave of His Son — to believe in the Lord Jesus Christ. A dead man cannot speak, and, of course, a dead man cannot believe, so we are in an equal difficulty. Praying and believing are alike impossible with the unregenerate man, without the quickening of the Spirit of God. The great point is to find out what we are commanded to do, what our duty to do. It is to tell every man the good news, and press him instantly to believe it. It is the Spirit that is the agent, but He always uses the truth as the instrument, the truth about a crucified and now risen Christ. Faith does not come by feeling, trying, nor praying, but by *hearing*. The moment I accept Christ as my own individual, personal Saviour who put away my sin, I am warranted to believe that I am born again, and the Spirit in the new man will lust against the flesh in the old man. Peace, indeed, I have with God, that is, Christ, but no peace with myself There is a faith that is human, and a faith that is Spirit-wrought. The plan is of God; the redemption, the truth, and the faith, are all of God. But how can I know whether I have God-wrought faith? Does my faith take hold of what is going on within? That is not of God. Does my faith take hold of, is it taken up with, what was done eighteen hundred years ago on Calvary, and with Him who suffered there? This is God-honouring and saving faith. This is being born of the Spirit. The Spirit introduces by the truth, Christ as the life into my dead soul. This is quickening, *the renewing* of the Holy Ghost. The Holy Ghost thus gives a *new* nature.

II. Indwelt by The Spirit.

In John iv. 14 we read of the indwelling of the Spirit ' as a well of water springing up into everlasting life.' This is said only of Christians. The Spirit of God dwells in none but in those whom He has quickened. And He *dwells* in all whom He has quickened (Rom. viii. 9). In some in greater measure than in others; but 'if any man have not the Spirit of Christ he is none of His.' Therefore, all who are Christ's have the Spirit dwelling in them. There is a danger here in *separating* Christ and the Spirit in us, as there is in regeneration of *confounding* Christ's work for me with the Spirit's work in me. It is as linked with Christ, a son as Christ is a son, an heir as Christ is, that the Spirit dwells in the believer, even as He dwelt in Christ, of course in Him without measure. It is thus we have *access*, for through Christ we have access by one Spirit to the Father. It is thus that we can *worship* the Father in spirit and in truth. This lesson he taught the poor confessed sinner at Sychar's well. It is thus that we are practically *sanctified*, more and more separated from evil, for He is the '*Holy*' Ghost, the 'Spirit of holiness.' It is thus we are *comforted and guided*; for Jesus said, If I go away I will send the Comforter (literally *paraclete*) which includes much more than comfort). This same word is used in i John ii. i, for Christ the advocate (literally *paraclete*) one who looks after all our interests. And thus, as Christ looks after all our interests before God, so the other *paraclete* looks after all our interests as we are passing through the wilderness, the divine Servant leading us into all truth; for here again the truth is His channel.

Thus we *live* in the Spirit (all Christians being dead and risen with Christ), and the exhortation is founded on this, 'Let us also *walk* in the Spirit' (Gal. V. 25), principally as being connected with Christ and the members of His body, in every member of which the Spirit dwells. We are to walk in the Spirit, in the practical exercise of brotherly love, and not be *walking as men*. What! are we not *men?* No; we are sons of God indwelt by the Spirit. Men walk in selfishness. The walk in the Spirit is each esteeming another better than himself

Thus we are 'led of the Spirit' (Gal. v. 18). All Christians are led. This is not an exhortation, but a privilege. ' For as many as are *led* by the Spirit of God, they are the Sons of God,' and all believers are sons. But though in each Christian the Spirit dwells, the exhortation is given, 'Be filled with the Spirit' as with the air you breathe, so live in the presence of glory, in the light, in fellowship with Father and Son, and thus the atmosphere will be 'the Spirit.' He is spoken of as

1. *A witness.* (i John v. 6.) He bears true witness. He tells the truth concerning Christ, He is a witness to Jesus Christ having come by water and blood; and every Christian has Him dwelling within him, as we also see in Rom. viii. a witness that we are sons. He is the witness of love and accomplished redemption.

2. *A seal.* As the goods are stamped by the purchaser after they are his own, so, after we believe, we are sealed. Only sons are sealed. The oil was put on the blood of the trespass offering. (Lev. xiv. 25, 28.) In the experience of many these go together; but many, especially in Apostolic days, though they knew their sins were forgiven, did not know they had eternal life. A quickened soul is not necessarily an emancipated soul.

3. *An earnest.* He is the earnest of our inheritance—that is, part of it that we possess now. The Israelites got the grapes from Eshcol while still in the desert. In Rom. viii. 17, we are children (the Spirit bearing witness), and as such sealed; 'but, if children, then heirs; heirs of God and joint-heirs with Christ.' Therefore, since He, as heir, has not taken the inheritance, we do not have it, but suffer now, having the earnest of the inheritance, until the redemption of the purchased possession. 'Ourselves also who have the first fruits of the Spirit, even we ourselves groan within ourselves, waiting for the adoption, to wit the redemption of the body.' (Rom. viii. 23)

III. Communicating the Spirit.

In John vii. 38, we read, 'He that believeth on Me, out of his belly shall flow rivers of living water.' Thus those who have been quickened, and who are indwelt by the Spirit, are now the channels through which He is ministered to others. The waters once flowed from a smitten rock. The water flowed from Christ's wounded side, and it is only as we are smitten, exercised, subdued, that these rivers will flow from us. Only as we come thus to Christ and drink, shall living waters flow from us. Alas! how little of the Spirit we see flowing from those professing to be quickened by the Spirit. Is it not because we are drawing little from the great fountain-head? 'Let him come unto Me and drink.' It is truly through saved sinners that God is now to send forth His river of life. 'The love of God is shed abroad in our hearts by the Holy Ghost.' And this love of God we are to pour out in rivers in this arid desert as witnesses of God; first, by carrying the gospel to our fellow-sinners, and telling of that Christ whom we know, and who is offered to them; and, second, by ministering love to all the saints of God in building up and comforting them. And it is only as our own affections and thoughts, that is, all our inner man, is filled with the pure water from the fountain, that the rivers can flow.

In connection with the three operations of the Spirit of God which we have been considering, namely, *quickened, indwelt,* and *communicating* we may look — ist. At Christ himself; 2d. At the Church corporately; 3d. At each individual believer,—

1st. As quickened by the Spirit.

Christ was born of the Spirit. This was His incarnation as we read in the angel's answer to Mary in Luke i. 35. 'That holy thing which shall be born of thee shall be called the Son of God.' (Luke i. 35.) The meat-oflering had to be mingled with oil. (Lev. ii. 4.)

The Church corporately in the *resurrection* of Christ. (Rom. i. 4; i Pet. i. 3.) He was quickened by the Spirit, as the head of the body, (i Pet. iii. 18.)

The *individual* believer; when the Spirit applies the truth to his conscience. (James i. 18.) ' Of His own will begat He us with the word of truth.

2d. Indwelt by the Spirit.

Christ we see sealed with the Spirit when at His baptism, the Spirit, as a dove, rested on Him. The meat-offering had to be anointed with oil (Lev. ii. 4.) 'Him hath God the father sealed.' (John vi. 27.)

48

The Church, we see at Pentecost, not merely quickened, but formed into a temple for God on the earth: the true temple, filled with the true glory. And we see this accomplished in fulfilment of Acts i. 8. ' Ye shall receive power after that the Holy Ghost is come upon you, and ye shall be witnesses *unto me* (1.) both in Jerusalem and in all Judea, (2.) and in Samaria, (3.) and unto the uttermost part of the earth. The Holy Ghost thus fell on,

1. The Jews, when they were *waiting in prayer* (Acts ii. 4), in obedience to Jesus' resurrection command, ' wait for the promise of the Father which ye have heard of Me.' (Acts i. 4.) They had heard of Him in John xiv. to xvi.

2. In Samaria, by the *laying on of the apostles' hands* (Acts viii. 17).

3. The Gentiles, in the *preaching of the Word* (Acts X. 44). And thus is the Spirit now given. In this latter method was the proper Gentile pentecost our pentecost. Thus it is in the preaching of the Word that we are to expect the blessing of the Spirit.

The *individual* is seen in his sealing: when by believing the record of the witness he receives his emancipation, his conscious liberty and peace with God, taking his place as a son, with the Holy Ghost as the testifier, and waiting with Him as the earnest of the inheritance.

3d. Communicating the Spirit.

Christ in His ministry and prophetic work communicated the Spirit.

The Church is seen communicating the Spirit, in the preaching of the apostles, at and subsequent to, Pentecost, in the Scriptures they have left, and all collective testimony from their day to this, that has been in accordance with the Word of God.

Individuals, in the outflow of love in our place, in the wilderness, as evangelists, teachers, pastors, or in any service to God.

[Each of these words, Born, Indwelt, and Communicating, has its opposite severally in the three words spoken about the Spirit, Resist, Grieve, and Quench.]

I. The Spirit may be *resisted.*

Acts vii. 51: ' Ye stiff-necked and uncircumcised in heart and ears, ye do always resist the Holy Ghost.' This is addressed to the unconverted who resist Him as a quickener.

II. The Spirit may be *grieved.*

Eph. iv. 30: ' Grieve not the Holy Spirit of God, whereby ye are sealed unto the day of redemption." This is addressed only to saved people, who can grieve Him as an *indwelling* Spirit. This shews what a friend He is to us. If you had committed some great sin, your mother would be grieved, your enemy would be rejoiced. You can grieve only a friend. What a touching appeal, fellow-believer! What will the consequence be? In love He will reprove, lie will rebuke our consciences, until we are consciously cleansed, and He can again dwell in us ungrieved.

III. The Spirit may be *quenched.*

I Thess. V. 19: 'Quench not the Spirit.' Many have been perplexed with this text, thinking that it had reference to the *indwelling* of the Spirit. You may grieve Him thus, but no believer can quench Him thus; 'For they shall never perish;' but the next verse, ' Despise not prophesyings,' explains it. A Christian cannot quench the Spirit in himself, but by refusing to allow Him to work from a fellow-Christian, he thus may quench Him. It is thus the Spirit in His communications who may be quenched.

As He can be resisted in His testimony which is His instrument in *quickening,* and grieved in His person as *indwelling,* so he can be quenched in His gifts as *communicating* life. If I despise the humblest channel that God has formed and tilled to dispense His streams of life, and put a sluice upon their flow, I stop His testimony, I quench the Spirit. It has nothing whatever to do with the indwelling of the Spirit. That can never be quenched; for the foundation of God standeth sure. But what a solemn warning in this day of self-seeking and pretensions! *Resist* is the word applied to the unconverted. *Grieve* is that applied to the individual Christian. *Quench* is that which has reference to the saints when gathered together, waiting on the Spirit.

The sin against the Holy Ghost has often been spoken about. All sin is against the Holy Ghost. What Christ spoke about in such solemn and awful words in Matt, xii., was 'blasphemy against the Holy Ghost,' and if the context is looked at it will be seen that this blasphemy consisted in giving Satan the credit of doing what was known to be God's work.

Bring your ignorance to the Holy Spirit, the great teacher, who by his -precious truth will lead you into all truth.

No, not the love without the blood;
    That were to me no love at all;
It could not reach my sinful soul,
    Nor hush the fears which me appal.

I need the love, I need the blood,
    I need the grace, the cross, the grave,
I need the resurrection-power,
    A soul like mine to purge and save.

The love I need is righteous love,
    Inscribed on the sin-bearing tree,
Love that exacts the sinner's debt,
    Yet, in exacting, sets him free.

Love that condemns the sinner's sin.
    Yet, in condemning, pardon seals;
That saves from righteous wrath, and yet,
    In saving, righteousness reveals.

Love boundless as Jehovah's self,
    Love holy as His righteous law,
Love unsolicited, unbought,
    The love proclaimed on Golgotha.

This is the love that calms my heart,
    That soothes each conscience-pang within,
That pacifies my guilty dread.
    And frees me from the power of sin.

The love that blotteth out each stain,
    That plucketh hence each deadly sting.
That fills me with the peace of God,
    Unseals my lips and bids me sing.

The love that liberates and saves,
    That this poor straitened soul expands,
That lifts me to the heaven of heavens,
    The shrine above not made with hands.

The love that quickens into zeal,
    That makes me self-denied and true.
That leads me out of what is old,
    And brings me into what is new;

That purifies and cheers and calms,
    That knows no change and no decay,
The love that loves for evermore,
    Celestial sunshine, endless day.

Heaven Opened!

Our Study

'So He drove out the man.' — Gen. iii. 24.

THE gates have closed that guard the way to the tree of life. The flaming sword turns every way, so that no flesh can approach and live. Man has sinned. God is righteous. Well might angels weep as they beheld such a sight. **Heaven is shut**. God dwells in his secret place. Thunders and lightnings are round about Him. Clouds of thickest darkness hide Him from man. The blood of Abel's Lamb, the rejection of Cain's first-fruits, attest the fact. Heaven is shut. The blood-sprinkled door-posts, the thousands of altars, the myriads of bleeding victims, the smoke ever ascending from the fires of judgment, the unceasing priestly work, all proclaim heaven's doors are shut

But *promise* shone through the dark cloud of *judgment,* and the glory of One coming to deliver was revealed; and while the captive Israelite sat in his desolation beside the ruins of Chebar he wrote, ' The heavens were opened, and I saw visions of God.' (Ezek. i. i.) Thus we see heaven opened concerning,

1. Christ In Prophecy.

And it is God who opens, it is God who shews the visions. The visions were about the glory of God and his relation to Israel, the cloud, the chariot of His glory then departing as with wings and wheels from His dwelling on earth. His ancient people are seen scattered and broken, but the heavens do not close (in vision) until again the glory of God fills the temple, and besides the whole earth is filled with His glory, and heaven and earth are finally united under the righteous sway of the Prince of Peace, the coming deliverer. May He hasten that glorious day!

2. Christ In Obedience.

But turn now to another scene, — Matt. iii. i6. In Jordan's waters stands a spotless, perfect Man, in the place where the godly Jews confessed sin in the baptism of repentance. Grace (not sin) has brought Him hither, that He might fulfil all righteousness, and when He came as the perfect servant in the sinner's place, 'Lo, the heavens WERE OPENED unto Him, and He saw the Spirit of God descending like a dove, and lighting upon Him; and lo, a voice from heaven, saying. This is My beloved Son, in whom I am well pleased.' This is heaven opening on Christ in obedience.

Jesus Christ was the only perfectly obedient man that earth has seen. Never had earth beheld such a sight, the glorious sun had never before risen on such a day. God is looking down from an opened heaven upon a Man, and on that Man His eye can rest with perfect satisfaction, perfect complacency. God declares Him to be His Son. As Man, He is anointed for His work with the seal of the Father. The Holy Ghost descends on the meek, the lowly, the obedient One. He Himself is the Person on whom the *heavens open*. The Father testifies of Him; the Holy Ghost testifies of Him; the eyes of the believing ones are turned towards Him. On no other object in this God-hating, God-rejecting world, could God's eye have rested. The Spirit, like the dove of Noah, looked over all the waste of waters, and found no rest but on the ark. He was the solitary witness for God in this world which He had made: so if the scene is an opened heaven and God looking down upon the earth, the sole attraction there is Jesus, the Son of God, the Son of man.

> 'It is the Father's voice that cries,
> 'Mid the deep silence of the skies,
> This, this is my beloved Son,
> In Him I joy, in Him alone.'

Again, we read of heaven being opened (John i. 51) in connection with

3. Christ In Government.

Here we have an intimation of the future righteous and peaceful government of earth united with heaven under the Son of man — where Jesus Himself says, 'Verily, verily I say unto you, here' after ye shall see heaven open, and the angels of God ascending and descending upon the Son of man.' Nathanael, the representative of the godly Jews, had confessed Him to be the Son of God and king of Israel; and Jesus now told him chat those who received Him, when He was on earth, should see yet greater things than those which had convinced him; and further, they should see *heaven open*, and He who had come down to be the *Son of Man* the Man of sorrows, should, in that name, be the object of the ministry of God's highest creatures. This will be true in all its fulness to those of Israel whom Nathanael represented, in a coming day. Meantime, we see heaven open, and all the ministry between heaven and earth carried on through Him. Our thoughts are taken back to Jacob at his ' Bethel' (Gen. xxviii. 12), where, from his pillow of stone, a ladder reached to heaven, on which angels ascended and descended, and we see Jesus uniting earth to heaven, for He has been raised up and set at His Father's right hand; and in Him we are raised from the grave of earth to the seats in heaven, quickened together with Christ, raised up together and made to sit in heavenly places in Him. The scene is changed, but the object to which all eyes are turned is the same. An opened heaven no longer looks upon the Son of God in humiliation, but upon that same Son of man uniting heaven and earth, God and His creature, and on Him as the object of the ministry of the angelic hosts. Blessed time for this poor groaning, misgoverned earth 1 Then will be known the full power of the Lord of hosts, who has said that He will 'open unto you the windows of heaven, and pour out a blessing, that there shall not be room enough to receive it' (Mal. iii. lo). Meantime, we gladly take rejection with Him, until He sits on His own throne, for if we suffer with Him, we shall reign. Our next spectacle of an open heaven is the sample of what an open heaven sees now on earth, and our place here under the kings of the earth who are plotting against the Lord and His anointed. Heaven is opened on

4. Christ In the Glory of God.

To the rejected disciple (Acts vii. 55). 'Stephen being full of the Holy Ghost, looked up steadfastly into heaven, and saw the glory of God, and Jesus standing on the right hand of God, and said, behold, I see the heavens opened, and the Son of man standing on the right hand of God.' Man had rejected Christ; God had taken Him to His own right hand. Man, in his most inveterate hatred of God, had sent out of the world the only Person in it on whom God's eye could gaze with complacency. Heaven can open now upon nothing on this earth. When it opens it is itself the scene; but the object to the mind of God, and to the believer full of the Holy Ghost, is still the same Jesus. Stephen was being sent after his Master. The Third Person of the Trinity in him was being rejected as the Second Person had been at the cross. The Son of man would still stand to return, until his testimony had been rejected; He is now set down waiting till His enemies are made His footstool. What a glorious sight to the believer in testimony, in rejection, in martyrdom I He sees not the stones, he hears not the derisive shout, he beholds not the fiendish gesture, ' he sees *heaven opened*.' (Heaven opened *on* Jesus; it opens *to* us.) So it is with us now: whatever enmity of men or devils may be around us, faith now sees heaven opened and Jesus at the right hand of God for us. It is no longer the eye of God delighting to look through an opened heaven upon His Son on earth, it is the Christian himself looking from earth into an opened heaven, and seeing all the glory of God, and better than all the glory, and above the highest of even God's heavenly glories, 'the Son of man,' there for him.

Never before had such a sight been seen, a glorified Man at God's right hand. Prophets had spoken of it — but here is the fact. Glory was native to heaven — but now we see the *Son of man* in the glory of God. What a gospel for every sinner, for every son of man, did Stephen preach, when, filled with the Spirit, he told out that heaven was opened, and the Son of man there! Is my reader a weak and trembling one, and can hardly dare to think that he is saved, and quite conscious that he has never been filled with the Holy Ghost? Listen to the glorious good news that God Himself has commanded to be told to every one: *heaven is opened*-— the veil is rent— God's hand has done it; not open now for God to look on us merely, but open for us to look upon God. The gates of Eden have been opened — Christ is the Door — and further, the *Son of man* is there. As Son of God He never required to leave, and go back to, that glory; but as Son of man He never would have been there unless God had been vindicated — God had been glorified in the putting away of sin — sin that lay upon man — the sin of the world. 'It is finished.' This is God's good news; a quickened sinner, an open heaven, and an exalted Substitute! This is the ground of my peace. Not what I *feel* —not the suppression of God-dishonouring thoughts — not success in the conflict — not growth in grace
— not the feeling of an indwelling Spirit — not a growing more like God — but the sure testimony of God to an open heaven and the Son of man before Him. What more do we need than what God has done? The tombs are rent as if to show that the sinner is to meet God now in life, in resurrection, therefore Stephen, a poor sinner,

stands filled with the Holy Ghost. The veil is rent to show that the way into the holiest of all is now made manifest, therefore, heaven is open to the believing sinner. The Lord is risen, and is at the right hand of God, and He is there the Son of man for me. An unveiled God, an opened tomb, a glorified Son of man — what more, dear trembling soul, do you want? The natural eye has never seen this; *faith* alone, by the Holy Ghost, beholds such a glory. Light from earth has never pierced the midnight darkness in which God is enveloped. The flaming sword still turns every way to guard ' the tree of life,' but where it fell; there is no entrance into Paradise but by the Door. There is no mercy to sinners but in Christ. The world knew not the darkness in which God wrapped His Son, when on the cross lie was dealing with sin. The last hour of light the world had was spent in wagging their heads at, and spitting upon the Light of Life. No un-quickened man saw Jesus in resurrection (Acts X. 41). Faith alone can see Jesus thus; the self-emptied sinner alone can rest, where God has found rest, in the glorified Son of man.

Again we see heaven opened. In Acts x. 11, Peter ' saw *heaven opened*, and a certain vessel descending unto him as it had been a great sheet, knit at the four corners, and let down to the earth.' Heaven is opened to explain the mystery of

5. The Church Formed.

The Church of God had been hid in God. It is not according to earthly and Jewish distinctions of clean and unclean. It is not according to the thought that the Moabite and Ammonite should not come into the Israelitish congregation of God. This was true (Neh. xiii. i) — is true, and ever shall be true. But, here is something new. The middle wall of partition is broken down, and there is neither Jew nor Gentile. This was never revealed nor prophesied about before. The Gentile was to be blessed, but mediately through the Jew, and that will yet take place. Peter saw clean and unclean on an equality, not the unclean benefited by the clean.   Those that were far off, and those that were nigh, that is, the Jews, nationally separated to God, and the Gentiles outside of God's calling, all now stand equally guilty, and equally to be blessed by God. To Peter had been given the Keys of the Kingdom (not of the Church), and he opened the door first to the Jews in his sermon in Acts ii. at Pentecost; and then, after this heaven-given vision, to the Gentiles, in the person of the centurion (Acts x. 44), and since the door has thus been opened, equally to both, no national distinction recognized, this key is no longer necessary. We now have the Holy Ghost sent down from heaven. This is the vision of the true dwelling place of God on the earth — the body of Christ. The middle wall of partition between Jew and Gentile was broken down, and His servants were sent to gather out of every nation, kindred, and tongue. His Church, which is to consist of all kinds of saved sinners, that in the ages to come ' He might show the exceeding riches of His grace.' May we be thus living on Christ, and thus doing His will — partners in His work of ingathering now, soon to be with Him in the glory above! For again do we see heaven opened on

6. The Church Seated.

'After this, I looked, and behold a door was opened in heaven. And the first voice which I heard . . . said. Come up hither, and I will show thee things which must be hereafter (Rev. iv. I, &c.).' In the apocalyptic vision, John had seen the Son of man in glory, as the first of the three great divisions of the vision (Rev. i. 19). He had also seen God's Church history — 'the things that are' — the second great division, in the history of the seven Churches (Rev. ii. iii.). And he is now to behold ' the things which must be hereafter' as the third division. But the Church represented in the throned elders has been caught up (i Thess. iv.), and is now seen seated with Christ on thrones (Rev. iv.) before all the judgment is poured out. They shall judge the world. They are like Abraham, the friend of God, apart from Sodom, hearing all that is to fall on Sodom. This is what we are waiting for to be caught up to meet the Lord in the air, and to be set with Him on His throne (Rev. iii. 21). What a contrast to the martyred Stephen! This is the Church triumphant, that was the Church militant. Well may we praise the Lord for this little glimpse into an opened heaven, for He would have our hearts to rest on the blessed thought that we shall be enthroned around the crowned Jesus, before He comes to execute His wrath. For this is not all: — Again heaven will be opened, not in the vision of prophecy, not on the meek, lowly Jesus, not on His suffering people, nor to show His calmly seated Church, but to show

7. Christ And His Saints in Judgment.

He comes with myriads of His saints. Christ with the Church is now seen rising up in the exercise of judgment, as John says in Rev. xix. II—' I saw HEAVEN OPENED, and behold a white horse; and He that sat upon Him was called Faithful and True, and in righteousness He doth judge and make war. His eyes were as a flame of fire, and on His head were many crowns: and He had a name written, that no man knew but He Himself And He was clothed with a vesture dipped in blood: and His name is called the Word of God (John i. i). And the armies in heaven followed Him upon white horses, clothed in fine linen, white and clean. And out of His mouth goeth a sharp sword, that with it He should smite the nations: and He shall rule them with a rod of iron; and He treadeth the winepress of the fierceness and wrath of Almighty God. And He hath on His vesture and on His thigh a name written KING OF KINGS, AND LORD OF LORDS.' Such is the awful opening of Heaven upon a God-dishonouring earth when the rejected, crucified Son of man shall disperse the mid-night darkness in which this earth is wrapped, by the flash of His judgment-sword. That funeral pall of blackest dye which has hung over this doomed world from the sixth hour of that most awful crucifixion day shall be torn asunder by His hand when He executes judgment. Then will be seen, not the deluge of water, as when, in Gen. vii. 11, the windows of heaven were opened, but wrath from heaven, the wrath of the Lamb. What a day! what a reality! The book of mere} closed! Christ risen

Up I the door shut! The sword unsheathed! How the scene is changed! No longer humiliation—-no longer angelic ministry — no longer His martyred followers; but His fierce vengeance — His own right hand — His own sword girt on His thigh — His now triumphant co-heirs riding forth in victory and breaking to pieces all before Him. Still the object is Jesus, the Word of God. For it is Christ Himself who is our study, let Him be on earth, in heaven, or joining earth to heaven, rejected or reigning, suffering or subduing. That same pierced brow which wore the thorny crown is now to be decked with many crowns, for,

'The crowns that are now round the false one's brow
Shall be worn by earth's rightful Lord.'

That same pierced hand shall draw the sword from its scabbard; those same wounded feet shall press the snowy clouds, and 'every eye shall see Him, and they also that pierced Him: and all kindreds of the earth shall wail because of Him.' God Himself breaks the silence; everything is now felt by every one to be real. The oft-rejected Christ is seen to be real; the scorned judgment is seen to be real; an open heaven is seen to be real; an eternal hell is seen to be real; the winepress of the fierceness and wrath of Almighty God is seen to be real; the wrath of the Lamb is seen to be real.

Flee from the wrath to come, and study Jesus who has opened heaven, and who is all the glory within an opened heaven.

Heaven was opened — Jesus came;
He revealed the Father's name.
   Took our place to bear our load,
God has owned Him from above,
Sent the Spirit, like a dove.
   Sealed Him and with Him abode. —
Matt. iii. 10

Heaven is opened— Lo! we see
Christ who died upon the tree
   Joining earth to heaven above —John i.
51.
   Angels, servants from the throne,
Blessings bring through Him alone:
   Richest tokens of His love.

Heaven is opened —glorious day
Jesus hath put sin away;
   Men of every tongue and race,
Jew and Gentile, bond and free,
All are welcome equally, — Acts x. ii.
   All may share God's matchless grace.

Heaven is opened — Christ has gone
Into heaven, His work is done;
   Him we follow, Him alone.
He whom men have crucified.
Son of man now glorified, — Acts vii. 55.
   Sits upon His Father's throne.

Heaven is opened —on the throne
See the One whom men disown— Rev. iv.,
xi
   Now the judge of quick and dead.
Lo! the temple, Christ the light,
He who by His wondrous might
   Bruised for ever Satan's head.

Heaven will open yet again— Rev. xix. 11.
We with Him shall judge and reign.
   Every eye shall see His face,
Proud rebellious men shall quail.
Nations, kindreds, all shall wail,
   All who scorned His truth and grace.

Triumph and Conflict

Our State.

AS SORROWFUL, YET ALWAYS REJOICING.' — Such was Paul's experience (2 Cor. vi. 10). The saved man is a great mystery to the unsaved; happy yet sad; triumphing, yet troubled; having no sin on him, and yet having sin in him; having no condemnation, and still having fearful conflict. Saved now, yet working out his salvation, and waiting for salvation. Even among saved men themselves there is great misunderstanding. Some are engaged more with the triumph side, others with the conflict side of a Christian's experience. We find both most fully brought out in Scripture, each having its own place and importance. The Christian's conflict takes rise and character from his triumph. We get much instruction by looking at the illustrations of a believer's triumph, walk, and conflict, as contained In the figures of the Old Testament; for we know that 'Whatsoever things were written aforetime were written for our learning, that we through patience and comfort of the Scriptures might have hope' (Rom. XV. 4). Let us look at Israel's history. We find the Israelites

1. Sheltered by blood from God's hand in judgment in Egypt and testifying for God in the midst of godlessness.
2. Redeemed by power. Taken through the Red Sea by the power of God's might and living by faith in the wilderness.
3. Entered into their possessions and in Canaan fighting the battles of the Lord. Let us look at these in detail.

I. —Sheltered by Blood.

The Israelite in Egypt.

The Lord spake unto Moses and Aaron in the land of Egypt, saying, ' This month shall be unto you the beginning of months: it shall be the first month of the year to you. Speak ye unto all the congregation of Israel, saying. In the tenth day of this month they shall take to them every man a lamb. . . . Your lamb shall be without blemish, a male of the first year. . . . And they shall take of the blood and strike it on the two side posts and on the upper door post of the houses wherein they shall eat it. . . . For I will pass through the land of Egypt this night, and will smite all the first born in the land of Egypt, both man and beast, and against all the gods of Egypt I will execute judgment: I am Jehovah. And the blood shall be to you for a token upon the houses where you are, and *when I see the blood I will pass over you*, and the plague shall not be upon you, to destroy you, when I smite the land of Egypt.' (Exodus xii.) In Egypt the Israelite had thus a triumph and had also a conflict.
1. *Triumph.* — He rejoiced because he trusted to the blood on the lintel, and to the word of his Jehovah God who had said, 'when I seethe blood I will pass over you.' So the Christian in this world rejoices, not in the thought that he is pure and sinless, but in the fact that Christ died for his sins. We see this fully explained in the Episde to the Romans, iii. 21 to v. 11.
God could pass over because the blood was on the lintel.
The Israelite could rejoice because he believed God.
Thus God can now justify the ungodly.

'When I see the blood I will pass over you.' (Exod. xii. 13).
Being now justified by His blood' (Rom. v. 9).

The believer can rejoice being at peace with God.

'The blood shall be to you for a token' (Exod. xii. 13).

57

Sheltered by blood, we feast upon the roasted Lamb with bitter herbs, unleavened bread, and in the pilgrim garb — at perfect peace, for 'it is Christ that died.'

> Heirs of salvation,
> Chosen of God;
> Past condemnation,
> Sheltered by blood.
Even in Egypt feed we on the Lamb,
Keeping the statutes of God the I am.
> In the world around 'tis night
> Where the feast is spread 'tis bright,
> Israel's Lord is Israel's light.
'Tis Jesus, 'tis Jesus, our Saviour from above,
'Tis Jesus, 'tis Jesus, 'tis Jesus whom we love.

2. *Conflict,* — There would have been *an un-scriptural conflict* in Egypt, if an Israelite had tried by any and every means to put off the hand that was crying for blood, except by God's own ordained means, the blood on the lintel; the acceptance of God's estimate of the value of the blood that He himself had appointed. This uu-scriptural conflict we find in modern times, in man's efforts by prayers and religiousness, and penances, and sorrows, to live a good *life,* when God is demanding the *death* of the sinner for his sins. And how often do we see the sad spectacle of a man in a condemned world trying to get up religion or devotion, or anything else to meet the wrath of God against his sins, when he is condemned already! This is the state of man as depicted in Rom. i. 18, to iii. 20.

But there is a *scriptural conflict* —namely, the conflict against

The World

The Christian presents a strange anomaly that cannot be seen perfectly in the figure of an Israelite sheltered by blood in Egypt. He has been taken entirely out of Egypt, and yet he is sent back to Egypt, as Jesus said to His Father in John xvii. 18, concerning His followers, 'As thou hast sent Me into the world, even so have I also sent them into the world.' According to the illustration, every Christian in one aspect, and a very practical aspect, is still in Egypt, that is the world which spiritually is called Egypt where also our Lord was crucified' (Rev. xi. 8). So Jesus prayed: — 'I pray not that thou shouldest take them out of the world, but that thou shouldest keep them fi-om the evil' (John xvii. 15). Being thus in the world and not of it, with souls saved, but with bodies still liable to disease and death, and all creation under the curse, 'We that are in this tabernacle do groan being burdened, not for that we would be unclothed but clothed upon, that mortality might be swallowed up of life ' (2 Cor. V. 4). And 'we know that the whole creation groaneth and travaileth in pain together until now. And not only they, but ourselves also which have the first fruits of the Spirit, even we ourselves groan within ourselves waiting for the adoption, to wit the redemption of our body' (Rom. viii. 23). These are groans which should not be stifled, but encouraged. The more that we are in harmony with the mind of God the more will these groanings be heard; not the groaning of an anxious soul to get peace, which God has already provided and presented, but the groanings of the saint who is waiting for his body to be fashioned like unto Christ's body of glory. This is evidently quite different from fighting against indwelling corruption. We are like the Israelites waiting till all the chosen of the Lord shall have actually had the blood on the lintel, which will be completed only when the Lord comes. We have been sent into this world to persuade men to come under the protecting power of the blood of Jesus, and thus be sheltered from wrath. Meanwhile our place is described in the 17th chapter of John where we find that the; Christian is

Given to Christ out of the world (ver. 6).
Left in the world (vers. 11 and 15).
Not of the world (ver. 14). »
Hated by the world (ver. 14).
Kept from the evil of the world (ver. 15).
Sent into the world (ver. 18).
Preaching the word to the world (ver. 20).

'God forbid that I should glory save in the cross of our Lord Jesus Christ, by whom the world is crucified unto me and I unto the world' (Gal. vi. 44).

II. —Redeemed by Power.

The Israelites In the Wilderness.

I. *Triumph.* — A quickened soul is first exercised about what *he has done*, — that he has sinned; and then, as we have seen, he gets peace, because forgiven through the blood of Christ who died for him. But he very soon finds out a further distress, not arising from what he has done, but from what *he is* — a sinner. This is described in Rom. v. 12, 'As by one man sin entered into the world.' He has been sheltered from God's hand in judgment, but he finds he requires a new life in which to serve God. The Israelites found themselves, after having been delivered from the death of their first-born, with *rocks* at either side, *foes* behind, and *the sea* before. So the Christian was born a sinner; his own sinful nature is unchanged and unchangeable; and the law of God is against him—three obstacles much more terrible than those of the Israelites. Many a quickened soul in such a case is ready to cry, ' Hast thou taken us away to die in the wilderness?' (Exod. xiv. ii.) 'Who shall deliver me?' (Rom. vii. 24.)

But God does not say, 'I have taken you away to die,' but He says, "*go forward*" (Exod. xiv. 15). God is for us, and His power is exercised through death, through the territory, the last domain of law. Man's extremity is God's opportunity. A way is made in the sea. ' The Lord saved Israel that day out of the hands of the Egyptians: and Israel saw the Egyptians dead upon the sea-shore ' (Exod. xiv. 30). This deliverance points not so much to Christ dying, as to Christ ' raised again for our justifica-

59

tion;' not to justification by blood, but ' to justification of life,' Rom. V. 18 (in Christ as risen from the dead): 'For if when we were enemies we were reconciled to God by the *death* of His Son, much more being reconciled we shall be saved by *His life*, that is His life in resurrection. Not only are we out of the house of bondage, but we are out of the land of Egypt. Every Christian has a right to say — 'Not only has God sheltered me by blood, but He has saved my soul by His power; not only have I peace with God, but God is for me; not only has God's hand been stayed from visiting me for my sins in wrath, but God's hand has been manifested in destroying all my enemies; not only am I not condemned, but there is no condemnation; not only did Christ die for me, but my standing is in Christ risen from the dead' (Rom. viii. i). 'It is Christ that died, yea, rather, that is risen again.' (Rom. viii. 34.)

> Pilgrims and strangers,
>   Captives no more;
> Wilderness rangers.
>   Sing we on shore.
> God in His power parted hath the sea,
> Foes all have perished, His people are free.
>   By the pillar safely led,
>   By the manna daily fed,
>   Now the homeward way we tread.
> 'Tis Jesus, 'tis Jesus, our Shepherd here below:
> 'Tis Jesus, 'tis Jesus, 'tis Jesus whom we know.

2. *Conflict.* — There is an *unscriptural Conflict* here also: — How am I as a sinner in the world, under law, to get out of my old standing in Adam and to get into the wilderness with God?

If the Israelites had tried to scale the rocky precipices on either hand, the barriers of nature, instead of taking God's way by a new and supernatural path altogether, this would have been an illustration of a quickened sinner trying to climb this mighty obstacle ' born in sin,' this mountain of his nature, instead of taking God's way out of it, as seen in Romans v. 19, 'As by one man's disobedience many were made sinners, so by the obedience *of one* shall many be made righteous.'

If the Israelites had turned on the foes behind, and had tried to fight their way through, instead of standing still to see the salvation of God, this would have been an illustration of a quickened sinner trying to fight against and extirpate his evil nature, or make it better, and thus try to get delivered from the wages of sin, instead of taking God's way in Romans vi. 23, eternal life through *Jesus Christ* our Lord.'

If a quickened sinner were attempting to get deliverance from the power of the law of God and its righteous demands, by trying to make that which cannot be subject to the law of God a willing servant, he should be as the Egyptians, trying to get through where faith alone could walk, which the Egyptians assaying to do were *drowned.*' That is the doom of man's efforts; but in Christ Jesus we have died, we have risen; Reckon therefore yourself dead indeed unto sin. It is not that we feel dead to it, or are dead to its motions; but as Christ died to it, so we reckon ourselves dead. Instead of crying therefore when I find such a holy law inoperative in bringing my God-hating nature into subjection, 'Who shall deliver me?' (Romans vii. 24) and stopping there, I look back on all my foes dead on the shore. Christ's grave is empty now, and God looks at me as in Christ Jesus, and every question of sins and sin is settled for ever. Christ, my sins, and myself, were all nailed to Calvary's cross. I believe this fact, that Christ is risen. I accept God's meaning which He has attached to this fact, that I am now not in my sins. I can now sing, in spirit, the triumph song of Moses on the wilderness shore of the Red Sea, and truly say, in the language of Romans viii., 'There is therefore now no condemnation to me in Christ Jesus, for the law of the Spirit of life in Christ Jesus hath made me free from the law of sin and death.'

But also a *scriptural conflict* now begins — namely, the conflict against

The Flesh.

This is not a conflict to obtain peace; not a conflict to get deliverance from condemnation, not even that sympathetic and God-honouring groaning of Romans viii. 18-28, but conflict against myself It is not the conflict against the world. If we look at Israel as the illustration, we find that there were no Egyptians in the wilderness, only Jehovah's congregation is there. We are now shut in with God: God's enemies are our enemies; we are on His side, even against ourselves. We have been crucified and raised; we have sung the song of victory; we triumph in Christ Jesus, and now we have conflict in earnest with our own evil natures. The man who realises that he has got once and for ever into the standing described in Rom. viii. i, 'There is therefore now no condemnation to them that are in Christ Jesus,' with all his triumph, realises tremendous deadly conflict, not around him, but within him, not struggling to get acceptance with God, but keeping his body under, looking at his own unchanged and unchangeably evil nature within him with something of the abhorrence of God—every day confessing his sin, every day requiring the Advocate. After the Israelites had sung the triumph song on the wilderness shore of the Red Sea, after they had received the pillar cloud to guide them, bread from heaven to feed them, and the water from the rock to refresh them, '*then* came Amalek and fought with Israel in Rephidim.' Does this not give us an illustration of the lusting between the flesh and the Spirit as seen in Galatians v. 17, 'The flesh lusteth against the Spirit, and the Spirit against the flesh, and these are contrary the one to the other?' This Ousting' or warfare goes on, not that we may cr}', 'O wretched man, who shall deliver,' but 'that ye may not do the things that ye would' (*lit.*). This is a tremendous personal reality in every saved man. At the same moment that he is rejoicing in Christ Jesus, he has no confidence in the flesh which is still actually within him, and thus he has a warfare every day against himself

Read Exodus xvii. 8-16, where we get the account of the conflict: Joshua, the captain of the Lord, fights with Amalek (son of Eliphaz, eldest son of Esau); Moses is on the hill-top with the rod, holding up his hands in intercession to God, supported by Aaron and Hur, one holding up each arm, for as long as his arms were held up Israel prevailed. And Joshua discomfited Amalek with the edge of the sword. An altar is raised, called Jehovah my banner, for the Lord will have war with Amalek, not once for all, but *from generation to generation*. This is all after the Red Sea has been crossed.

This gives us an illustration of how the Spirit of Jesus fights against the flesh. The Advocate is with the Father on high, and He is Jesus Christ the righteous, the spotless High Priest, making continual intercession for us. The Spirit overcomes the flesh by the Word of God. This is all after we have joyfully sung the victory-anthem recorded in Romans viii. ' There is no condemnation to them that are in Christ Jesus.' And indeed we have a specimen of the mighty sword we are now to wield by the Spirit in us in the practical exhortations laid down in the last chapters of the epistle to the Romans, commencing with chapter xii.

As the Israelites found that the sword of Joshua and the prayers of Moses routed the heathen Amalek, so the Christian finds that there is nothing like the truth of God, the authority of God, the sword of the Spirit, accompanied by the intercession of Jesus on high for the unsubject flesh within him. All the wilderness conflict has this character: 'Thou shalt remember all the way which the Lord thy God led thee these forty years in the wilderness, to *humble* thee and prove thee, to *know* what was in thine heart, whether thou wouldst *keep* His commandments or not.' (Deut. viii. 2.)

Beloved brethren, 'seeing then that ye are risen with Christ, mortify therefore your members which are upon the earth.'

We have triumph because we are forgiven. We have conflict because we sin.

We have triumph for we are saved. We have conflict because we are sinners, although saved.

We have triumph over our Adam-nature, for we are not in Adam, but in Christ. We have conflict within us, for, alas I we often 'walk as men.'

We 'are not in the flesh,' therefore we have triumph. The flesh is in us, therefore we have conflict.

We are 'not under law' therefore we have triumph. Jesus said, ' If ye love me, keep my commandments,' therefore we have conflict. We are not *under law*, neither are we *lawless*, but we are *inlawed* — that is, *under authority*, or duly subject to Christ.

Christ has taken charge, not only of our salvation, but of our conflict and our walk. Grace saves, but Grace also teaches. Neither is it by an internal power only that we are guided, but by external authority or commandment. We do not walk in the paths of righteousness, merely because *we see* them to be righteous, but because God has *ordered* them. The former would be self-pleasing, the latter is God-pleasing, and if ever the question should arise between what I feel and see to be right and what God says is right, then I must obey God rather than my own feelings. Abraham did not understand how it was right to sacrifice his son, but he believed God, and offered his son because God told him.

As long as the Israelites were in the wilderness, they were seen in themselves, as needy and sinful, while God was proving himself bountiful and gracious. We find a wonderful illustration of God's provision for the Christian's need very near the end of the Israelites' march. In Numbers xxi. we have a sad pidhire of their murmurings, and at verse 6 we read, ' The Lord sent fiery serpents among the people, and they bit the people; and much people of Israel died. Therefore the people came to Moses, and said, we have sinned, for we have spoken against the Lord, and against thee; pray unto the Lord, that he take away the serpents from us. And Moses prayed for the people. And the Lord said unto Moses, make thee a fiery serpent, and set it upon a pole; and it shall come to pass, that every one that is bitten, when he looketh upon it, shall live. And Moses made a serpent of brass, and put it upon a pole, and it came to pass, that if a serpent had bitten any man, when he beheld the serpent of brass, he lived.'

As long as the Christian is in this world, he will have sin in him, and his power against it is Jesus crucified. The Son of Man lifted up on the cross is what withers up practically and daily our rebellion, waywardness and perversity, and in Him God sees no iniquity in Jacob and no perverseness in Israel. And if we say we have no sin, we deceive ourselves, and the truth is not in us.

III.—Seated in Heavenly Places in Christ Jesus.

The Israelites In Canaan.

I. *Triumph,* —Israel under Joshua got through the Jordan, as Israel under Moses got through the Red Sea. All Canaan was theirs, 'From the wilderness and this Lebanon even unto the great river, the river Euphrates, all the land of the Hittites, and unto the great sea, toward the going down of the sun, shall be your coast.' (Joshua i. 4.) This was the land flowing with milk and honey; the land in which they were to have long life and prosperity; the land wherein they were to dwell and be fed. The Israelites were blessed with all temporal blessings in earthly places in Canaan. Of us, as Christians, now it is said: God '*hath* blessed us with *all* spiritual blessings in heavenly places in Christ.' Certainly, we have many blessings which we never think of, and never have thought of, but we can think of none which we do not have in Christ. Every Christian has Christ—nothing less. He may not know all: who does? We strive that we may know Him, that we may grow in grace, and in ' the knowledge of our Lord and Saviour.' In Christ every Christian is blessed with every spiritual blessing in heavenly places.

He is quickened, raised, seated already in heavenly places in Christ. Therefore, according to the illustration, he is in Canaan as to his triumph; for as Christ is so are we in this world. He is dead, risen, seated, so are we in Him. (Eph. i., ii., iii.)

    Canaan possessors,
      Safe in the land.
    Victors, confessors;
      Banner in hand.
Jordan's deep river evermore behind,
Cares of the desert no longer in mind.
    Egypt's stigma rolled away,
    Canaan's corn our strength and stay,
    Triumph we the live-long day.
'Tis Jesus, 'tis Jesus, the Christ of God alone;
'Tis Jesus, 'tis Jesus, 'tis Jesus whom we own.

2. *Conflict.* —There is an *unscriptural conflict* here, as we have seen in Egypt and the wilderness. This conflict is said to be (Ephesians vi. 12) 'not against flesh and blood.' There is more in this simple statement than might at first appear. We are in the world; we are not of it. Our work is not to fight to put the world right. This is the

mistake of all who have taken, or may take, the sword to fight the Lord's battles in this dispensation. We are here to act in grace as children of the Father, and to save men from the world. Our enemies are spiritual, not men in the flesh. We are not sanctified Jews, praying the 109th Psalm, and slaying men, women, and children. That was the right thing in Canaan; it is the wrong thing in the places in which we stand, not only as far as bloodshed, but the principle goes down to every wrestling with the weapons of this world. Have I been cheated? what is my remedy? Go to law? Nay. But then I shall suffer loss. Very well, suffer (i Cor. vi. 7; I Pet. ii. 20). The believer is done with all 'flesh and blood' conflict. He may be called a fool, a mad-man—one that has no interest as a citizen, as a politician, a person of Utopian ideas and transcendental schemes. He is content so to be styled, and moreover is not to retort. His life is hid with Christ in God. All contact with the world's ways can but defile him. ' Flesh and blood' is not the platform on which he wars. World philan-thropists he may admire; world reformers he may be thankful for; but he hears his Master say, 'Let the dead bury their dead' (if decently buried, so much the more agreeable for us), 'follow thou me.' But there is a scriptural conflict, namely, the con-flict against

The Devil.

All Canaan was given to Joshua; but we read that they had to enter in and take possession of it personally — 'everyplace that the *sole of your foot shall tread upon* that have I given unto you' (Joshua i. 3). They had to fight for every inch of the land. First Jericho fell, then Ai, until Joshua routed his thirty-one kings. Read Joshua xii. And after we are told that we are already raised and seated in Christ, that we al-ready have been blessed with all spiritual blessings in heavenly places in Christ, the conflict is put before us in the very heavenly places where we are blessed, as Josh-ua's fighting with Canaan's kings was in Canaan.

This conflict is not against the world nor the flesh — we have considered these already — but it is against Satan the accuser, wicked spirits ruling the darkness, demons that hate the light (Eph. vi. 12).

1st. What are they? 'Principalities and powers.' They possess strength of evil, strong wills, more powerful than ours. They originally derived strength from God, and their apostate will rises from themselves.

2d. What do they do? They have *power* over the world as governing it; for it is in darkness, and they are ' the rulers of the darkness of this world.'

3d. Where do they dwell? They *dwell* 'in heavenly places,' and thus ever endeav-our to obtain a religious and delusive ascendency over us, for they are ' spiritual wickednesses.' And what do we require for these foes who dispute our possessions. This is not Pharaoh keeping us in bondage; not Amalek fighting with us, but the Ca-naanites disputing our own possessions. The former two we were saved from; the latter we have to meet in their true attitude, as keeping us from our rightful place as the redeemed of God. We fight, clad in the armour of God. ' Be strong in the Lord, and in the power of his might. Put on the whole armour of God, that ye may be able to stand against the wiles of *the devil.* For we wrestle not against flesh and blood, but against principalities, against powers, against the rulers of the darkness of this world, against spiritual wickedness in heavenly places. Wherefore take unto you the whole armour of God, that ye may be able to withstand in the evil day, and having done all to stand. Stand, therefore, having your loins girt about with truth, and having on the breastplate of righteousness; and your feet shod with the preparation of the gospel of peace; above all, taking the shield of faith, wherewith ye shall be able to quench all the fiery darts of the wicked. And take the helmet of salvation, and the sword of the Spirit, which is the word of God: praying always with all prayer and supplication in the Spirit, and watching thereunto with all perseverance and supplication for all saints' (Eph. vi. 10-18). This is neither to 'get peace,' nor to avoid condemnation, nor to get into ' heavenly places.' It is not with the judgment of God, nor the law of God, nor sin within me. This conflict is against the wiles of the adversary, who, day and night, tries to deprive me of all that God has given, and all that faith enjoys.

Let us see how air this bears upon us. Some look upon a Christian as out of Egypt, now in the Wilderness, and waiting to reach Canaan. This may have some truth in it, but it does not convey the whole truth as to our position.

Others look upon it thus:—We are in Canaan by faith: we are in the Wilderness in fact; and we may be in Egypt, Wilderness, or Canaan as to experience. Again, there is truth here, but I do not think it is exactly put as subsequent Scripture warrants. Let us shortly sum up all the above:—

Heb. xi. 28-30.

I. — 'Through faith he (Moses) kept the passover, and the sprinkling of blood, lest he that destroyed the first-born should touch them.'
Exod. xii. — Rom. v. 1-11. Triumph by blood.
John xvii. — Rom. viii. 22-28. Conflict with the world.
II. — 'By faith they passed through the Red Sea as by dry land, which the Egyptians assaying to do were drowned.'
Exod. xiv. 10; XV. — Rom. viii. Triumph in power. Exod. xvii. 8-16. —Gal. v. 17. Conflict with the flesh.
III. — 'By faith the walls of Jericho fell down after they were compassed about seven days.'
Josh. i. — Eph. i. — Triumph in our inheritance.
Josh. xii. — Eph. v. — Conflict with the devil.

'All these things happened unto them for types, and they are written for our admonition' (i Cor. X. 11). "By *faith,* therefore, according to the above parallel, we are *in Christ,* who is far above all Egyptian judgment, all Wilderness weariness, or even all Canaan conflicts. In actual *fact* we are still in the world; and in individual *experience* we have still clouds and sunshine, joy and sorrow, storm and calm. Thus there are three things the Christian has to distinguish: 1st, his Standing; 2nd, his State; 3rd, his Experience,— His standing before God, his state in this world, and his own experience as he passes through this world.

1. The Christian's Standing.

All Christians are by faith in the eternal calm of God, having everything that the work of Christ has secured. We are far above all principalities and powers in Him who is alive for evermore, who is the Living One, and was once dead. We are as near to God as Christ is, for we are made nigh by His blood; and we are as dear to God as Christ is, for Jesus, speaking to His Father, says, ' Thou hast loved them as Thou hast loved me' (John xvii. 23). In Him we possess all the fulness of God. But as to fact, we find another side of the truth, which is,—

2. The Christian's State.

According as we look at it, all Christians are still in *Egypt*. Not an enemy is really destroyed. The *world* is around us and against us. We are sheltered by blood, and still we are in a condemned world. We are eternally justified, and by grace we are saved persons; still, in plain English, in Scripture language, we are just where we were as to our surroundings.

Again we are, as to fact, still in the *Wilderness*, requiring guidance by the eye of our Father every day. As the Israelites of old had no sign-posts nor highways in the trackless desert, and were guided by the pillar-cloud, so human wisdom and human advice can never direct the Christian in his heavenward journey. God's word is His light. As the Israelites had to get their bread daily from heaven, marching through a barren wilderness, so the Christian gets no food for his new nature in that which his fellow-men all around him enjoy. He says, 'The life which I now live in the flesh, I live by the faith of the Son of God, who loved me and gave Himself for me' (Gal. ii. 20). Every day the Israelites required the water from the Rock in the dry and parched land, so the Christian daily drinks the truth of God. Christ is his daily re-freshment. These are for our *weariness.* The Israelites likewise had Joshua to light, and Moses to pray, against their foe Amalek; so we have the Spirit to war against the flesh, and our advocate with the Father. Jesus presents the blood for us on high, and daily we require our feet to be washed from all earthly defilement. These are God's provisions for our *sin.*

Again, as to fact, we are in the *Canaan* conflict, following our Joshua through all his wars, which are our wars. Every Christian is really, as to fact, in Egypt, in the Wilderness, and in Canaan, at one and the same time. Different aspects may be more prominently ours at one time than at another, and this constitutes experience. The experience of Christians is not always Christian experience.

3. The Christian's Experience.

What do we find the every-day experience of Christians to be? According as a Christian understands what his standing is and what his state is, so will be his expe-rience. But every Christian's experience must be 'a walking with God.' He may be, as to experience, sheltered by blood, and hardly knowing it, like an Israelite in Egypt not realizing the safety that there was under the blood-sprinkled lintel. He may be consciously at peace with God by the blood, but still trembling under the fear of coming into condemnation, like an Israelite not seeing the path through the sea, and trembling lest Pharaoh's host destroy him; but he will be walking with God up to the light that he has. He ma}' be rejoicing on the solid ground of Christ risen, having for ever done with all against him, and having God now for him consciously, and he thus walks with God, like an Israelite passed through the Red Sea, and entered upon the wilderness journey. And, finally, he may be walking as in heavenly places, like an Israelite through the Jordan and settled in Canaan. He is God's workmanship, and is now getting into the mystery of His will (Eph. 9), having lost sight of the thought of his own salvation, and being absorbed in God—as the aged pilgrims have told us, that for years they had never had a thought about their own salvation—as the aged Bengel said, 'The same old terms.' And it is only when in conscious experience we have been taken thus far, that we can study God for his own sake and for what He is. This is the furthest we can reach here.

The *standing* of every believer before God in Christ Jesus, known only by faith here, is the same, and is independent of his realising it or enjoying it.

The actual *state* of every Christian upon the earth is likewise the same. What an anomaly any Christian is in the world! A son of God walking through a God-hating world, with a God-hating devil its head, and having within him a God-hating nature; the fact being that every Christian, as to conflict down here is in Egypt, in the Wilderness, and in Canaan.

The *experience* of every Christian is not the same, but varies in different people, and in the same person at different times, according as he knows his standing before God, knows his state and walks in the Spirit. Thus we find the reason of so much seeming contradiction in Scripture, and in the writings of God-taught men. I am sometimes confronted with a passage in a man's writings, and asked, ' Do you believe that?'

'Yes,' I answer; 'and do you believe that?' — a directly opposite statement (seemingly), and again I say,—

'Yes,' because I find the same expressions in God's Word.

They all reconcile themselves in our own consciousness, if we are submissive enough to wait and learn God's mind. I wish that you, my Christian reader, may distinctly see the difference between what the Christian is in God's sight, and what he is in this world, and also why there is so much difference in different Christians. There is one path, and but one path, in which our God and Father would have us walk; that is the path of His own Son here in conscious sonship witnessing for Him as if we were in Egypt, the Wilderness, and Canaan, taking sides with Him against the world, against ourselves, and against the devil. This is Christian experience; but, alas! this is not always the experience of Christians. This may depend upon their not rightly dividing the word of truth, or their not seeing the truth in its many aspects. If we draw up a few seeming contradictions from God's word concerning the Christian in parallel columns, if we read down one of them we shall find the experience of some Christians; if again we read down the other, we shall find the experience of another class of Christians — but Christian experience is the harmonious and scriptural blending of both. (I wonder what angels think as they see such sons of God here!) Did not Paul know this strange contradiction. I saw an infidel tract the other day meant to prove the Bible to be false, by drawing up in parallel columns about a dozen contradictions found in Scripture, such as, 'Whosoever is born of God 'sinneth not,' and, 'If we say we have no sin, we deceive ourselves,' &c.; and I thought, 'Are the infidels really so far back?' so I commend the following four dozen, instead of one, to their notice, and promise more when these are understood. The poor infidel never heard of a new creation and an old in the same man. He knows only the old, and patches

Well-known.	Yet unknown.
Behold we live.	Dying.
Always rejoicing.	Yet sorrowful.
Making many rich.	Yet poor.
Possessing all things.	Having nothing.
Ye have put off the old man.	Put off all these.
Ye have put on the new man.	Put on therefore.
Who can be against us?	World, devil, and flesh.
Who shall lay anything to our charge?	The Accuser accuses the brethren day and night.
Who is he that condemneth?	We judge ourselves.
He that is born of God sinneth not.	If we say that we have no sin we deceive ourselves.
We are not in the flesh.	As long as we are in the flesh.
Not under law.	Keep my commandments.
He that believeth in the Son hath everlasting life.	We live if ye stand fast in the Lord.
The Lord's freemen.	Christ's slaves.
Being made free from sin.	Blood cleanseth (not has cleansed) us from all sin.
Accepted in the Beloved.	We labour to be accepted (in service).
We are not in the flesh, but in the Spirit.	The flesh lusts against the spirit, and the spirit against the flesh.
God who always causeth us to triumph.	What great conflict I have for you.
We are already saved.	We are working out our salvation.
	We are waiting for salvation.
Let us therefore as many as be *perfect*.	Not as though I were already *perfect*.
Ye are *complete* in Him.	We pray that we may stand *complete* in all the will of God.
Seeing ye have *purified* your souls.	Let every one that hath this hope in Him *purify* himself.
Ye are *unleavened*.	Purge out the old *leaven*.
Father who hath made us *meet* to be partakers of the inheritance of the saints in light.	When He shall appear we shall be *like* Him.
Always confident.	With fear and trembling.
Through death He destroyed Him that had the power of death.	The last enemy that shall be destroyed is death.
Everywhere and in all things — To be full, and	
To abound, and	To be hungry.
Dead to sin.	To suffer need (Phil. iv. 12).
Risen with Christ.	Let not sin therefore reign.
	Mortify therefore your members which are upon the earth.
I am strong.	When I am weak.
We have an anchor sure and steadfast.	Make your calling and election sure.
They shall never perish.	Lest I should be a castaway.
Why as though living in the world.	The life which we now live in the flesh.
I am dead.	Nevertheless I live.
We are sanctified, justified; Christ our sanctification.	We pray that we may be sanctified wholly.
Seated in heavenly places in Christ.	We are in the world.
Bear ye one another's burdens.	Every man shall bear his own burden.
Your bodies are the temples of the Holy Ghost.	I know that in me (that is, in my flesh) dwelleth no good thing.
Saved from sin.	Chief of sinners.
Justified by faith.	Justified by works.
Sanctified by blood and will of God.	Sanctified by the word and Spirit.
Saints by call.	Purified by progress.
We (Christians) shall not come into judgment.	We (Christians) must all appear before the judgment seat of Christ.

All these seeming contradictions are thoroughly explained when one sees the difference between our standing and our state. If I reckon my standing according to my state, I am in a low and God-dishonouring experience. If I bring the power and character of my standing to mould my state, then I shall have a happy and God-honouring experience.

Soon faith will be fact. May our blessed Lord grant it. Not at death will this be true of the whole Church of God, but when He returns. Our experience will then be both what faith and fact are; our state shall then be as oui standing; our standing shall be our state. We shall then be ' like Him,' soul and

The Lamb on the cross has purchased all.	The Lamb from the throne, when He returns in power shall claim all, and actually take all.
In Egypt it is the blood of the Lamb.	Romans and Galatians shew us the power that brought us out and keeps us in Egypt.
In Amalek's fight it is the blood of the Lamb who is the advocate on high, that is presented.	Hebrews look at the Christian as always in the Wilderness.
It is by the blood of the Lamb that the accuser of the brethren is overcome. Clad in God's armour we fight.	Ephesians is the book of our Canaan.

body. Do we not long for the time when the last of the bride shall be under the shelter of the blood-sprinkled lintel, and we shall be caught up together from a doomed *world,* — when the last conflict with Amalek shall have been fought, and his remembrance blotted out for ever; the *flesh* for ever left; ' sins and iniquities remembered no more for ever;' when the accuser of the brethren shall have been cast out of the heavenly place, and every opposing *spiritual wickedness* shall have been routed; when our Joshua, by His judgment-warfare (Rev. iv. to xxii.), shall have cleared the inheritance. Then, in the splendour of the Lamb on the throne, we shall be manifested as the sons of God, the body of Christ, the bride of the Lamb.

Fellow Christian, are you making your experience the standard for your walk? This is wrong.

Are you making your state your standard? This also is wrong.

But God would have us make our standing our standard. This honours Him. This gives conquering power.

Our attitude now is to wait calmly for the hour when all will be ours, in fact and also in experience, which is now ours in faith only; when our standing shall be our state. Even the Apostle Paul has not yet all; he is waiting with the Lord for what he was waiting for while here, — ' not to be unclothed, but clothed upon, that mortality might be swallowed up of life.' (2 Cor. v.) This is why resurrection, not death, is our hope—why we wait for the Lord's coming for us, and not for our going to Him. We do not wait for happiness merely, we wait for what will bring to a close this great paradox between *standing* and *state,* and also terminate that unseen state of disembodied souls with the Lord in Paradise. 'Even so, come, Lord Jesus.' 'Beloved, now are we the sons of God; and it doth not yet appear what we shall be: but we know that when He shall appear, we shall be like Him; for we shall see Him as He is. And every one that hath this hope in Him purifieth himself, even as He is pure.' *(i John iii. 2.)*

The world, the devil, and the flesh give you conflict. The Father, the Son, and the Holy Ghost give you triumph.

Praise the Lord with hearts and voices,
   Gathered in His holy name;
Every quicken'd soul rejoices,
Hearing of the Saviour's fame.

Praise the living God who gave as,
   Lost and ruin'd as we lay,
His beloved Son to save us,
Bearing all our sin away.

Praise the Lord for all His guiding,
  Snares so thickly round us lie;
We in His own light abiding,
  Are directed by His eye.

Praise Him for His long forbearance;
  How our sin His heart must pain;
Righteous is His loving-kindness,
  Cleansing us from every stain.

Praise Him, enemies assail us,
  As we through the desert go;
But His sword can never fail us,
  It shall silence every foe.

Praise Him for the manna given.
  Falling freshly every day;
Jesus Christ, our Lord from Heaven,
  Is our food through all the way.

Praise Him for the water flowing,
  Freely in its boundless tide;
Christ the smitten Rock we're knowing,
  Pierced for us His wounded side.

Praise Him through the desert marching,
  Onward to the golden shore;
For our Saviour we are watching,
  And we'll praise Him evermore.

'Under the Sun.'

Our Walk.

Ecclesiastes.

IN reading the book of Ecclesiastes I have been struck with the frequent occurrence of this expression, *'Under the sun.'* It occurs twenty-nine times in this book of ten chapters, and is nowhere else in the Bible. ' Under the heavens ' is thrice mentioned, and ' upon the earth' four times.

I have met Christians who have been sadly perplexed by several expressions in this book which seem so contradictory to other parts of the Scripture. Infidels have also exultingly brought some of its detached sentences as sanctioning their blasphemies. Legalists and Unitarians have quoted some of its precepts as proving their man-exalting and God-dishonouring doctrines. Worldly professors use its verses as a warrant for their worldliness, and an excuse for their practices.

That expression, *'under the sun'*, is the thread on which the whole book is crystallized. If we remember this, we shall have not the slightest difficulty in meeting infidel opposition or world-hearted profession. Solomon was the wisest as he was the richest king, trying all that was *'under the sun.'* The Holy Spirit has, in these few chapters, with divine accuracy, given us his experience, and ' what can the man do that cometh after the king?' He had plenty of money, and all the resources where men think pleasure is to be found ' under the sun'—wine, music, works, vineyards, gardens, orchards, fruit trees, water-pools, servants, possessions of cattle, silver, gold, peculiar treasures, men-singers, women-singers, musical instruments of all sorts — in short, whatever his eyes desired he kept not from them (chap. ii.). A better collection could not be brought together for any man ' under the sun.'

And with all his enjoyment he still kept his wisdom, as he says, 'yet acquainting mine heart with wisdom.' But in such multiplied sources of pleasure did he not tarry too long at the enjoyment of one side of his nature, and leave some other corner untried? Nay; he found a season for everything. For loving, for hating, for laughing, for weeping, for dancing, for mourning, for all he had a time. He saw that after all he had tried *'under the sun'* he was no better than a beast; for as we look at a man and a beast *'under the sun*,'' a common grave shuts out the light of the sun equally from the horse and his rider.

It is *'under the sun'* that the outward eye sees, and if the things seen are all that we are to have, there is nothing better than what Solomon says— ' Behold that which I have *seen*: it is good and comely to eat and to drink, and to enjoy the good of all his labour that he taketh under the sun all the days of his life, which God giveth Him; for it is his *portion*.' The *things seen* give eating, drinking, and enjoyment of labour as the only portion. This is the highest good, according to what was seen by the greatest philosopher as looking at things *'under the sun.'* He was also a great student. Read i Kings iv. 33.

As to the higher part of man, we find a wonderful text in Eccl. ix. i: ' No man knoweth either love or hatred by all that is before him.' No; we have to look above us for love and hatred, not before us, that is to say, in this world. By what is before us we are asked to remember our Creator, but are never turned to our Redeemer. Hence, *'under the sun'* we find men scarcely dare rise above the names Creator, Providence. And when we do remember this great Creator, as creatures under His sun, we find that the conclusion of all, the ultimate limit we can reach, is to know His demands upon us; as His demands in their own place and nature on a tree or an animal; His demand on us as creatures,— the whole duty of man, which no man ever did or can do, is to 'fear God and keep His commandments.'

This wisest and richest man found *'under the sun'* no profit in all his labour; nothing new; wicked men in judgment; oppression of the right; folly and wisdom going to the same end; chance seeming to regulate all; many sore evils consequent, notwithstanding what he says in i Kings v. 4: 'The Lord my God hath given me rest on every side, so that there is neither adversary nor evil occurrent.' In short, he found the beginning vanity, the middle vanity, the end vanity. The sum of all 'under the sun' —vanity of vanities.

How complete is the change when we turn to contemplate Him who comes from far above the sun, who created the sun and the earth, and descended to the earth from His rainbow-circled throne. When Christ came. He did not reveal the name 'Creator;' it was the name 'Father.' Christ was the last test of all *'under the sun'* The whole world has now been brought in guilty before God. Man's duty was to receive Christ, instead of which he gave Him a cross.

God is love, and God was manifest in the flesh; perfect love, perfect light. Eternal life has been here from above the sun. Hatred against sin has been seen, as nowhere else it can be seen, when, made sin for us, the sinless One drained the cup of the wrath of God. Love for the sinner has been seen, as nowhere else it can be seen, in that 'God so loved the world that he gave his only-begotten Son, that whosoever believeth in Him should not perish, but have everlasting life.'

A sister who had realized her position as witnessing for Jesus, and had come to understand what is meant by Solomon's time for everything ' under the sun,' wrote about a marriage party at which she had to be present. After describing what happened, she said, 'We then left very early, leaving the gay party to practise Solomon.'

We that have believed in the Son have got a most strange and anomalous position *'under the sun.'* 'As He is, so are we in this world.' As the Son of man dead, risen, and now in heaven in the fulness of His Father's love, so are we in this world. We have nothing whatever to do with what is *'under the sun,'* beyond getting through this world as simply as possible. ' If ye then be risen with Christ, seek those things which are above where Christ sitteth on the right hand of God. Set your affection (it is literally mind, as in the passage 'who *mind* earthly things') on things *above* — *not* on things on the earth, for ye are dead, and your life is hid with Christ in God.' All this is intended to draw us away from what is under the sun to what is *above*, even to Jesus Himself What is the occasion of all the worldly walk of so many professing Christians? We are not asking what the originating cause is. There is a difference between the originating cause and the occasion, sometimes called the predisposing and exciting causes. The originating or predisposing cause is found in this, that all Christians have in them the old Adam nature, unchanged and unchangeable, which lusts against the new, which abhors the things unseen and the walk by faith, which feeds upon the things seen, feasts on and revels in this present world. But there are several occasions or exciting causes which stir this old nature into conformity with the world. Let us look at three of the chief occasions of worldliness:

1st. Ignorance of self.
2d. Ignorance of what the world is.
3d. Ignorance of what God says about that world.

I. Ignorance of Self.

Christians not being aware of the worldly-minded foe within is a very common occasion of worldliness. They come nearer and nearer to the world, thinking themselves safe, and still doing nothing wrong, not knowing that it is like bringing gunpowder near the fire. If Christians would realise that they have a nature within them that feeds upon God's dishonour, they would be more watchful and prayerful. Every Christian has within him a traitor which loves the world, its ways and its principles, in some shape or other; a traitor which, but for the power of an ever present Spirit, would surrender the keys of the citadel at once to the world outside; a traitor which is not subject to the law of God, nor indeed can be; a traitor which is not to be trifled with, far less trusted; a traitor which is ever planning and scheming for its own gratification, and which is capable of anything evil. Christian! watch and pray against this foe within, as well as against foes without. Every Christian has the flesh still within him, which is a traitor against God.

II. Ignorance of What the World Is.

When we do not know what 'the world' is, we are very prone to slip into worldliness before we are aware. Some profess not to be clear upon what is worldly. They know, however, the meaning well enough of getting on in *'the world.'* Some look at '*the world*' as that which is glaringly wicked, or God-dishonouring in other people. The poor man speaks of the rich man in his grand house as being in the world, or the great man who never thinks of God. While all this may be true, every man has his 'world' into which he is tempted to go: the meanest as well as the greatest, the most secluded as those in the centre of a great city. A pretty ribbon or a new dress, a good dinner or a nice party, may be as much '*the world*' as the gayest and most fashionable assembly.

Often the question is asked, Is it right to go here or there? to do this or that? Is this of '*the world*' or not? God has given us a perfect criterion: 'All that is in the world .... is not of the Father, but is of the world.' This makes all plain to a child with the Father. Is this of the Father? If not, it is of the world. How well every Christian understands this in some measure! Does the size of your world not increase just in proportion as you know the Father? Things are now classed under the title 'world' that were not thought to be worldly when we started the race. The road gets narrower as this thing and the other thing are seen to be of ' the world till we are walking in the lonely path with the lonely Man.

Fellow-Christian, do you not see something this year to be of '*the world*' that you did not see last year? Have you been thus learning the Father? Is it a sign that the Father is being known more when we hear of professing Christians, yes, even deacons, elders, pastors, countenancing the worldly meeting, the gay assembly, or the dancing party? And where is the harm? is asked by many a voice. Ask at the entrance of many a fashionable gathering, '*Is this of the Father*? ' and you will get the contempt that your presence there deserves. For the world loves and knows its own: your presence asking such a question would be an intrusion.

This spirit of the world is paralysing the whole of Christian energy, as it is leavening the whole of Christendom. No wonder that there is a slumber as of death over our land, an unaccountable nightmare resting on the spirits of many Christian men, a feeling that we are just at the awful pause before some fearful explosion. Christians take the world's ways and party strifes in its politics and rule, blunting the edge of their spiritual nature, harming their conscience, condescending to mingle in the world's battles. Let the potsherds of earth strive with the potsherds thereof Where are the garments unspotted by the world? Christians also are mixed up with the world's company, sitting at the world's table, happy with the world's joys and jokes, singing the world's songs, and their bleeding Lord hanging at their side, each worldly thought or action doing dishonour to Him.

Young disciples are especially liable to be carried away with the cultivated, respectable, educated, quiet, polite, agreeable, pleasant, worldly companion. Young disciples, in the name of Him who hung on Calvary for you, keep no company with any unconverted person. You may have to meet them at school or in business, but never keep company with them. ' Come out from among them and be ye separate.' A young disciple was once asked concerning a companion, —

'Well, was she a friend or an enemy?'

'In what way?'

'A friend or an enemy to Jesus?'

'I really could not say.'

'But you know that all are either friends or foes; there is not a third company. Is she converted?'

'I don't think so.'

'Then, of course, we know to whom she belongs. Let us be friends to all Jesus' friends, and enemies to all Jesus' enemies — loving them, praying for them, and trying to get them converted, but coming out from among them and being separate.'

My brother, will that cross, will that bleeding One, not draw thy thoughts, thy words, thyself, away from this cruel world? Let them quaff their wine, let them chorus the revel song, let them have their time to dance. They are *'under the sun.'* *'Under the sun'* He died for thee. That sun was darkened when He was thinking of thee. He loved thee. Thy name, as an individual, was in His omniscient mind, when in darkness and agony He was forsaken of His God. Nails and a cross never kept Him there. He Himself made that iron and that wood, but love kept Him on the cross. Thou hast said, ' He loved me, and gave Himself for me.' His cross, His grave, separate thee from *'the world,''* as they separate thee from thy sins. Dost thou realise that every unconverted man is reckoned by thy Lord as a murderer? that this world is under the charge of murdering the Lamb of God?

In this land, at this moment, it is difficult to know the *church* from the *world.* The world, 'of the earth earthy,' has said to the Church, the bride of the Lamb, of the heavens, ' heavenly,' 'Come a little down to us, and we will rise a little up to you, and we can shake hands and agree.' This in the present day is called *liberality, charity, large-heartedness,* and he who dares to dissent is called a bigot, one of peculiar views, a man of extremes.

'The world' makes its social gathering and invites the Christian. A compromise is effected. The Christian leaves at home his peculiar testimony for his rejected Lord. ' The world ' lays aside a little of its open worldliness, and they thus agree. ' The world ' has been raised somewhat. Its tone has been elevated. The Christian has come down from his high standing ground, and has lost his place as the separated one — His Lord is dishonoured, and this is modern liberality! The world and the Christian agree, and God's name, God's glory, the offence of the cross, are given up as the price of the agreement!

Yea, some have shown their ignorance and heartlessness so much as to bring in Christ's example, and make his conduct a cloak for their worldliness, and the Holy Jesus a minister of sin. True, no one was ever such a friend to the sinner as Jesus, and no one was so separate from sinners. Did he contract any defilement by sitting and gating with sinners? It would be blasphemy to think it. Can you perfectly manifest Jesus wherever you go? But the rule here, as everywhere, is perfect and simple, ' Whether, therefore, ye eat or drink, or whatsoever ye do, do all to the glory of God' (i Cor. x. 31). Do you keep company with that friend because it is for the glory of God? Do you accept that invitation to dinner because it is for the glory of God? or not rather because you will enjoy it, and perhaps meet some one you like, or something else for you, and is this following Jesus? Not a word did he speak, not a thought did he think, not a step did he take, but was for God's glory. Not a company he entered, but this was his *only* reason for going. Is it yours? Let conscience answer. And if you can go on with worldly people and in worldly ways, either you will reap daily and bitter sorrow, and have to come in broken and contrite spirit to the footstool of grace, or you have no heart for the crucified one. You know not the Christ whom the world crucified. You are not Christ's one. You are not a Christian!

At this present day there is nothing that is leavening Christendom more evidently than this worldliness — worldly policy, worldly ways of advancing the cause of Christ, worldly principles, worldly maxims, worldly motives, worldly vindications of conduct, worldly schemes and artifices, gll are employed, and worldly arguments are finally adduced, shewing that all such are quite in proper place.

The spirit of competition, which is ' the life of trade,' has been adopted in those unchrist-like divisions in the Church of the living God. Artifice and trickery with world-shows, bazaars, and suchlike, are used to extract money from the pockets of willing and unwilling victims to advance God's kingdom! the Lord all the time loving the cheerful giver. But cheerful or not cheerful, the worldly church principle is, the money must be obtained! [Read *Babylon's great bazaar*, Revelations xviii. 12 and 13— gold at the head of the list, souls of men at the foot—not very unlike what may be seen in Christianised Britain!

In the mixture of world and church of this nineteenth century in Britain, who could discern the Bride of the Crucified One? Everything goes on comfortably. There is little of the taking up of 'the cross;' many excuses for conformity to this world.

I heard not very long ago of one who, standing very high in 'the Church' as a leading and devoted Christian, at a marriage party publicly announced that such a season was for enjoyment, and that such enjoyment should take the form of singing songs, &c.; holy hymns and such-like were not appropriate. Certainly it was the time for enjoyment. And if 'any man is merry, *let him sing psalms.'* But this does not suit modern mixtures of 'Church' and 'world,' fashionable Christianity!

Religion, with its psalms and hymns and spiritual songs, may do all very well for Sunday; for solemn times; for deaths or for funerals; for prayers, morning and night, at family worship; but for enjoyment, for merry-making, let us have a worldly song, or some foolish love-sonnet, before all the means that God has ordained as the channels for our joy!

This is what is called *intelligent* Christianity. 'Rejoice' is the motto of such men, but they forget *'in the Lord.'* Man's songs, man's dancing, are their channels of joy — 'psalms, hymns, and spiritual songs,' God's channel. The judgment-day will try all. Beloved fellow-Christian, rejoice now as you would look back from your death-bed with satisfaction and say, ' 'Twas not of the world.'

In travelling by rail, take out your Bible and quietly begin to read for your own instruction, in the presence of your fellow-passengers, and you will quickly observe that eyes are upon you in strange wonder—the eyes of those, too, who wish to be called *Christians,* but who cannot understand any man reading the Bible for *enjoyment.* The Bible, they think, should be read as a duty; but a piece of trash, in the shape of some yellow-boarded novel, or some new article of man's folly, is much more palatable and enjoyable. Dear reader, are you getting much enjoyment from the reading of the bare Word of your Father? This will fill you with His ideas, and displace your own. This will show you that there is much more *'of the world'* than perhaps you dreamt of; that all *'under the sun'* is equally vain for instruction or for enjoyment. This leads us to the consideration of the third occasion of this most deplorable and painful, though too common spectacle, of worldliness in a Christian.

III. Ignorance of What God Says About the World.

God alone knows the world thoroughly. There are three words in Scripture translated world; *1st,* Kosmos, which literally means the world in its perfect order and arrangement, as opposed to chaos; *2nd,* Aion, which literally means a period of time, an age; and *3rd,* Oikou-mene, literally meaning the inhabited world.

Especially with the two first have we at present to do. What could be more beautiful than the arrangement of this perfectly ordered world —the cosmos that God brought out of chaos: The world, in this sense, in itself is not evil; but its rightful Lord has been crucified, and therefore in this age, or dispensation, or period of the world, all must be away from God. By and by all things in heaven and in earth shall be gloriously under the one head, Christ, when the cosmos, the beautiful world, will appear in purer glory than in its pristine beauty, when it shall be not the present age, but the day of the Son of man,' ' the age to come' (Heb. ii. 5). Meanwhile the trail of the serpent defiles all. Its beautiful dells, and mountains, and plains, are polluted by the presence of men in rebellion against a holy God, and the unavenged blood of its martyred Lord is lying on it calling aloud for vengeance.

When the Spirit of God begins the practical exhortation to the Romans, in the 12th chapter, the first command of detail, after presenting our bodies living sacrifices, is, ' Be not conformed to this world;' that is, ' be not conformed to this age? Until a man knows this foundation-principle he cannot go on to the other related duties. Be done with the spirit of the age. Why? Because the age is under Satan, who is the God of this age (2 Cor. iv. 4). Its rulers are the rulers of the darkness of this age (Eph. vi. 12). And Christ ' gave Himself for our sins, that He might deliver us from this present evil age, according to the will of God and our Father' (Gal. i. 4). The cause of Demas forsaking Paul was that he 'loved this present age' (2 Tim. iv. 10); and earth's wisdom is not the study of the Christian, for we do not speak ' the wisdom of this age, nor of the princes of this age' (i Cor. ii. 6).

Christ our Lord and Saviour alone we own to be King of kings, but in this age the devil is prince of this world (John xvi. 11); and he declared this to Christ, the only true King in Matt. iv. 8, when he said he would give Him all the kingdoms of the world. The Creator was in the world made by Him, and the world did not know Him, but hated and crucified Him. The wisdom of this world is foolishness with God, and its power weakness. 'We have received not the spirit of the world, but the Spirit which is of God' (i Cor. ii.). And God has chosen the foolish things, the weak things, the base things of this world as His own vessels.

My reader, listen to God's own word—'Know ye not that the friendship of the world is enmity with God? whosoever, therefore, will be a friend of the world is the enemy of God' (James iv. 4). Would you not rather be on terms of friendship with that noble lord, or great man *in this world*; on speaking terms with those that the world loves to honour? And have you made up your mind for the guaranteed consequence? Thou art an enemy of God. ' Love not the world, neither the things that are in the world. If any man love the world, the love of the Father is not in }Iim' (i John ii. 15).

A man is known by the company he keeps, by the books he enjoys. Do you not enjoy a nice worldly dinner-party, where there is nothing very evil done, but all the events of the world discussed, much better than attending two or three prayer or worship meetings in a week? Have you made choice of the alternative? The love of the Father is not in you. 'They are of the world, therefore speak they of the world, and the world heareth them' (i john iv.5). 'We know that we are of God, and the whole world lieth in the wicked one' (i John v. 19).

My reader, pause and think. Are you deceiving yourself? Do you love *the world?* If, as before God, you cannot deny it, then the love of the Father is not in you. You go to church; you are very respectable on Sundays and week-days; you are honest, and charitable, and kind; but you love the world. Your feasts and solemnities ai _ an abomination unto God. You cannot force yourself to hate the world. It is natural to love it. By your love you prove that you have not the nature in you that abhors the world; that therefore, you have not been born again, but have been deceiving your-self I would solemnly advise you, before God, to begin from the beginning by getting converted. Cain was the first to try to make the world comfortable apart from God. God made him a vagabond. He built a city. He was the father of all the great world-improvers, with their harps and organs. No doubt they had made themselves very happy; no doubt they had their music and dancing; perhaps oratorios on the dying words of Abel, or the taking up of Enoch, as the 'Messiah' and 'Elijah' now-a-days. Having considered these occasions of worldliness, let us consider—

IV. The Place of a Christian Under the Sun.

Read John xvii., and there we find, —

First. At verse 9, Christ says, ' I pray not for the world, but for them which Thou hast *given* me: As given by the Father to Christ, we Christians are separated from this world by the eternal gift of the Father, and by the intercessory prayer of the Son. Mingling with the world, we break through that wondrous chain that Jesus became a man to form; we do despite to the Father's purpose, we trample on the prayers of the Son.

Second. In verses 11 and 15 we are spoken of as left in the world: ' I am no more in the world, but these are in the world.' And as He is, so are we. Are we living His life, reproducing Christ here as those that are left to do so? He was the light while here; we are the light of the world during His absence. Brother, did you ever feel lonely because Jesus was not here, because you have been left? Are you mingling with the world? You do dishonour to that heart which reckoned on your love while left here.

Third. Hated by the world: 'The world hath hated them,' because the world hated Him. Many Christians are persecuted for their own sake, and not for righteousness' sake. Christians may be hated for their own disagreeable ways; but are you hated for your likeness to Christ? He said, ' they hated Me without a cause.' Do they hate you because you manifest His holy name? Are you mingling with the world? If so, you are trying to escape the hatred, yea, you are silently consenting that the world did right in hating your gracious Redeemer.

Fourth. 'Not of the world,' verses 14 and 16. This is the cause of the former. The world loves its own. We are citizens of heaven. Heaven is our Fatherland. Heaven is our home. Heaven is our metropolis. We are foreigners here. We are like the Abyssinian captives, while they were in the chains of the king of that country. A few moments more, and, beloved fellow-captive, the chains shall fall, and we shall neither be in nor of the world. We are not of it, just as Jesus was not of it. A homeless, lonely stranger, the great Sojourner had ' not where to lay his head.'

We are here under protest. We protest against the awful power that the world-rulers have used in former days, and not one of whom has publicly protested against, namely, Pilate's boast, ' I have power to crucify Thee.' We glory in this, that we are identified with the murdered Man. Are you mingling with the world? By so doing you are denying your fatherland, you are ashamed of your citizenship.

Fifth. Ver. 15. While left in this world we are kept from the evil in it. Are we to rush near the evil from which our blessed Lord prayed His Father we might be *kept?* Are we to break through a Father's love, a Father's watchful care, and join the ranks of the aliens? Do we search at the broken cisterns, and thirst again for more and more of the music and dancing *'under the sun'* while we are those that are *kept?* Tremendous evil! All the more tremendous because, unseen and unrealised, it is around us, and from it we have to be kept. Nothing but Jesus' constant prayer, and the Father's constant, untiring love, could keep us.

Sixth, Ver. 18. We are sent into the world. As Christ was sent, so are we. We must be out of a place before we can be sent into it. The cross took us out of the world. We were crucified to it. In resurrection-life we are sent back to it, to be here as specimens of saved sinners, resurrection-men, stranger-witnesses, men that cannot be understood, men whose life is hid with Christ in God. Are you mingling with what is *'under the sun?'* If so, you deny the resurrection of Christ, and your resurrection with Him, and that you are sent into the world, and have to maintain your character as one who has been thus sent.

Seventh, Ver. 20. We are to *preach* to the world. All that are to be saved will be so by the instrumentality of saved men, sinners like themselves carrying the word of life to the dead. There is a strange infatuation in some men's minds, that because we are in the world to do the Lord's work, that therefore we must become somewhat assimilated to the world in order to get to its level! But the Christian is 'a light.' Light does not do its work by assimilation with darkness, but by opposition to it. The Christian's power in carrying the Word to a dead world is not in becoming like the dead, but in manifesting his new life, going to dead sinners with the omnipotence of God, and preaching His resurrection gospel, and not schemes of reformation, nor anything else except this gospel, knowing that the 'gospel is the power of God.' The Christian's wisdom is not that which schemes and plots for success according to worldly tactics, but in direct opposition to all; seeming to be downright foolishness. Saul's armour looks very strong; David's sling and stone seem quite contemptible.

We do our duty to the world only as we keep our Nazarite separated character. We shine brightly only as we oppose the darkness. We benefit mankind only as we glorify God and testify for the Crucified One. We are despised by man and chastened of God if we mingle with the world and 'blow hot and cold.' Christ spues out of His mouth the lukewarm.

'I am not a man of extremes,' says the *beau-ideal* of modern fashionable Christianity. 'I wish you were either cold or hot,' says God. Let God be true, and every man a liar.'

Let us 'make the best of both worlds,' says man. 'If any man love the world, the love of the Father is not in him,' says God.

'Secure friends here, and still keep a hope of heaven hereafter,' says man. 'The friendship of the world is enmity with God,' says God.

'Let us take our time for everything here *"under the sun,"* — dancing, laugh ter, amusements, comfort, position,' is man's creed. ' If any man will come after Me, let him deny himself, and take up his cross and follow Me,' is what God says. As you sow you shall reap.

'Truly the light is sweet, and a pleasant thing it is for the eyes to behold the sun; but if a man live many years, and rejoice in them all, yet let him remember the days of darkness, for they shall be many. All that cometh is vanity. Rejoice, O young man, in thy youth; and let thy heart cheer thee in the days of thy youth, and walk in the ways of thine heart, and in the sight of thine eyes; but know thou, that for all these things God will bring thee into judgment' (Eccles. xi. 7-9). — Man, who shall live for ever, giving up his eternity for present pleasure, giving up Christ for the world, is like one who is colour-blind, that is, like a person who can see well enough his way through the world, but cannot distinguish between red and green, or any other of the beautiful hues' that are seen in the rainbow. They that see colour in all its beauty and diversity, as God has made it, cannot but think it a great misfortune for those who cannot distinguish one colour from another. They see the crocus and the snow-drop the same as the green grass, and it again as the stone wall. Everything to them is either black or white, and the glorious rainbow is not distinguished from the black cloud that it spans. Everything is to them like an engraving, and the lilies of the field, that we are asked to consider, have no more beauty than is derived from their shape and position. It is a misfortune, but the unfortunate one does not know his loss. How true is that saying of Sir John Herschel, referring to this colour-blindness: '*What we never knew - we never miss!*" How true in the great realities of our existence! How many people go about this world absorbed in its business, its pleasure, or its science, and have never seen the most glorious sight that ever burst upon it — the perfect love of God to sinners, and the perfect hatred of God against sin; or rather, have never seen the most glorious Person that ever trod this earth as the sacrifice for their sin, as their propitiation, as the object to fill their hearts now and for ever!

They never knew Him, and they never miss Him. If you were saying, 'Christ is not in the world, do you miss Him?' the idea would startle many. Others would feel that they would not at all like Him to be always where they were; they would not feel free if He were always sitting at their table, or went with them wherever they went. Have you never heard people say, when a godly man had left their company, ' Well, I'm glad he's gone; we couldn't do anything before him? ' How would you like Christ to be always beside you? Far from missing Him, you are really very glad He is not here. Thank God there are those who have known Him, that do miss Him, and are waiting for Him. Why does the lady of the world so enjoy company, while the pierced Christ is never missed? Because she never knew Him. Why do the men of the world enjoy their learning, their riches, or their pleasure, and do not miss Christ,

God's greatest gift? Because they never knew Him. They wonder that people can enjoy prayer-meetings, gospel preachings, or Bible-readings, and always enjoy them — ready for them in the morning, at noon, or evening. They pity such. Is it not like the man who is colour-blind, pitying us as we stand in rapt enjoyment admiring the glorious rainbow? He feels the rain falling, but can see and admire no rainbow. We see the magnificent colouring of the rainbow, and forget the rain. They never knew the joy of being the Lord's, therefore they never miss it. And what is left in the world after Christ is taken away? He once was here, and God looked on Him well-pleased; but man in his blindness crucified this only worthy object on earth, and what is left? God has told us ' All that is in the world ' —

1st. 'The Lust of the Flesh.'

2d. 'The Lust of the Eye,' and,—

3d. 'The Pride of Life.' There are no other motive powers in the world but these. This trinity is reigning in power to-day as in the days of John the apostle.

1st. *'The lust of the flesh.'* — This has to do with the things by which the senses, taste and touch, and all merely animal gratifications, are nourished. This is the lowest and most universal. Rich and poor equally are under its power. What shall we eat, what shall we drink? Such do not eat to live, they live to eat, to enjoy themselves, to satisfy all the fleshly lusts that war against the soul. Thus we read of those that 'walk after the flesh, in the lust of uncleanness,' who serve 'divers lusts,' lewdness, wantonness. This is why tipplers and drunkards enjoy the world, till they forget name, business, wife and family, body and soul, for drink, which is the front door admitting to every other lust of the flesh. A man may be under the lust of the flesh who is not a drunkard, but who wishes to enjoy himself on this side of his nature.

2d. *'The lust of the eye.'* —This has to do with the senses of seeing, hearing, and so on. Here the man has not only desires, but means to gratify them. What shall we see? Some new thing, some new Vanity Fair. The Athenians would listen to anything new, quite kindred to this lust of the eye. This is the second motive power in the world. What will please the eye and tickle the car? This is what finds its craving satisfied in theatres, pantomimes, operas, concerts, sentimental and comic songs. They are all of one class: something that will satisfy their powers of *investigation* as the lust of the flesh has to do with the senses of *enjoyment*. This is even carried into the worship of the church; for what is ritualism but the lust of the eye? The lust of the eye is here gratified with gorgeous dresses, childish paraphernalia, sacred imitations of a pantomime, all accompanied by the solemn notes of worship performed on a splendid and solemn machine for making sound, worship done by proxy, to which the worshipper listens and worships by another, and for which he pays. And then people, conclusively to prove it, say, ' But we so enjoy it.' Of course. The lust of the eye is just the eye gratified. ' But wasn't the theatre very entertaining and grand?' Of course, and whenever Satan fails to make such things attractive, he must try something else for the lust of the eye. 'Turn away mine eyes from beholding vanity' (Ps. cxix. 37).

3d. *'The pride of life.'* —This is not what shall we eat? nor what shall we drink? nor what shall we see? But how- shall we be seen? Wherewithal shall we be clothed? What is the modern evening-party, and even a good deal of modern church-going? Either the lust of the eye or pride of life — either the lust to *see* or *to be seen*. How can I be thought to be great? How can I make a noise in the world? — How grand can my parties be, and excel all others? This requires, seeks, and obtains the opportunities lot display. How can I reach the pinnacle of earth's fame? How can I be a great scholar? How can I be a great preacher? How can I be anything great? I know such and such great men. I know Lord so-and-so, and am intimate with Lady so-and-so. These are some of the sentences of 'the pride of life.' Bengel says this pride of life ' is that which leads forth lust abroad, and diffuses it more largely into the world, so that a man *wishes to be as great as possible*,' in goods, in dress, in plate, in furniture, in buildings, in estates, in servants, in his retinue, in his equipage, in his offices.'

Is not one or other of these the key-note to the heart of every man in the world? Are these not what all your friends, relatives, and yourself, by nature have pleasure in? Perhaps they do not like one, but they will have another. How am I to get out of it? As long as I am 'of the world,' I cannot but get what is in the world. God says there is nothing in the world but these. You say you have Christ. Is he enough? If you ask such a question, you never knew Him, you do not miss Him. Suppose the lust of the flesh, the lust of the eye, the pride of life, were out of the world. I guarantee that its millions would miss them. Suppose good dinners, good parties, good theatres, thrilling novels, good worldly amusements, and greatness in something of the world were gone, many would miss them and be miserable without them. But they are all doomed, and all that enjoy them. 'The world passeth away, and the lust thereof, but he that 'doeth the will of God abideth for ever.'

Let us see how man got this threefold rope bound round him, and how he is to get it broken. He got it in the first Adam. It is broken when he gets into the second, then he is not of the world nor of what is in it.

The First Adam's Failure

(Introducing the Principles of the World.)
1st, 'The tree was good for food.' This was the *lust of the flesh*.
2d, 'Pleasant to the eyes.' This was the *lust of the eye*.
3d, 'A tree to be desired to make one wise.' This was the *pride of life*.

The Second Adam's Victory

(Overcoming the god of this World.)

1st, 'Command that these stones be made bread.' This was the *lust of the flesh*, overcome by the Word, ' Man shall not live by bread alone, but by every word that proceedeth out of the mouth of God.'
2d, ' The Devil *sheweth* Him all the kingdoms of the world, and the glory of them, and saith unto Him, all these things will I give thee if thou wilt fall down and worship me.' This was the *lust of the eye*, overcome by the Word, ' Thou shalt worship the Lord thy God, and Him only shalt thou serve.'
3d, Being set on a pinnacle of the temple. 'Cast thyself down: for it is written He shall give His angels charge concerning thee.' This was the *pride of life*, overcome by that Word, 'Thou shalt not tempt the Lord thy God.'

'This is the victory that overcometh the world, even our faith.' We live upon what is unseen. It is your time, we say to the worldling. Go on in the world with all it has, the lust of the flesh, the lust of the eye, and the pride of life. It is .-ill the heaven you will ever see. We can well bide our time, for this is all the hell we shall see. Especially to young disciples is the exhortation needed, ' Love not the world.' Their tendency is to the world; the warmth of nature, and the vigour of youth, drag the young Christian downward. His only safety is in total separation from the world.

He is not called to retire to a monastery. Jesus prayed not that we should be taken out of the world, but kept from the evil of the world. It is as really a sin to become a nun or a hermit as it is to mingle with the world. The Christian is to be like the fishes that were clean: they must have scales and fins, the scales to keep out the water, and fins to steer through it. He is not to be taken out of the world, but .to go through it, and keep from all that is in it, ' enduring as seeing Him who is invisible.' The world sees no beauty in Him; they do not miss Him, because they never knew Him. They are totally blind to what He is. Not so the Christian. His Saviour is Christ. His life is Christ. His object is Christ. This world is a wilderness, because all that is in it has nothing of Christ. Dear fellow-sinner, tremble at your enjoyment of earth's stores. Shall you ever know the only One worth knowing? You do not know Him now: 'What we never knew we never miss.'

Know Him above the sun, and you will soon understand what is meant by 'under the sun.'

Away from communion and walking with God,
Man entered his own way and death's path he trod;
'The world' in its course to destruction rolls on,
With vanity stamped on all *'under the sun.'*

In Eden, at Sinai, at Calvary's cross,
The world has been tried; all its glory is dross;
Man's failure at each step since time was begun
Has brought in as guilty all *'under the sun.'*

Condemned by our God even now in this world,
The stroke of His wrath soon 'gainst men shall be hurl'd ',
Yet still with his dancing to wrath he will run,
And try to find rest in all *'under the sun.'*

But God has determined lost sinners to save,
To bear all our burdens His own Son He gave;

He bled for our sin, and the work is all done,
God offers Him now to all *'under the sun.'*

As one with Him now we are seen on His Cross,
The fame and the fortune of earth are but loss;
We died in the death of the crucified One,
His grave severs us from all *'under the sun.'*

The mad world may revel in mirth o'er Him slain,
For this is their heaven, their god is their gain;
The sun clad in darkness. He died all alone,
And bore all our hell when thus *'under the sun.'*

On Christ throned above our affection is set.
From whence He shall come in His glory so great,
The last battle fought and the victory won,
His saints are caught up from all *'under the sun.'*

'No Confidence in the Flesh.'

Our Sanctification.

Do you know what in a Government would deserve a vote of *want of confidence?'*

'Indeed, I have little to say in politics on one side or the other, but there is a government against which I would with all my heart give a vote of *no confidence.'*

'What is that?'

'The government of an evil heart within, which is ever striving for the reins of power.'

'I agree with you; this is first: self-government is man's first duty.'

'I find that the evil heart, or "the flesh," as it is called in Scripture, is branded by the Holy Ghost with this mark, "No confidence." Look at Phil. iii. 3. Three steps may be seen in that wonderful passage —

1st, Worship God in the Spirit;

2d, Rejoice in Christ Jesus;

3d, Have no confidence in the flesh.

God is seeking worshippers — those who can worship Him in spirit and in truth. This is no legal drudgery, nor the vain attempts of mon to get into favour with God. You hear people, converted and unconverted, speaking of going to worship God. How could an unconverted man worship in spirit and in truth, when he neither has the Spirit in him nor has come to the Truth? and this alone is true worship. It is no mere routine of Christian duties —- singing, praying, preaching, or hearing; but it is the outflow of heartfelt adoration to God — it may be in silence, or in song or thanksgiving, but it is giving God back something, giving back His own gift, thinking God's thoughts about Christ.'

'And how can this high step be reached?'

'The Spirit's method is by making us "rejoice in Christ Jesus." No man can worship acceptably unless his joy is in Christ Jesus. In fact, worship is the overflow back to God of the full cup of joy. Why is there so little true worship? Because there is so little rejoicing in Christ Jesus. I know some are considered great authorities who would hardly dare to say they are saved, and call it presumption in those who do so; and I have often wondered what such think of this text, "Rejoice in Christ Jesus." A brother truly remarked that many Christians' Bibles should be printed, "Mourn in the Lord always; and again I say, mourn." "Rejoice in the Lord always" is as really a command as "Thou shalt not steal;" and our blessed Lord said, "If ye love Me, keep My commandments." Hence we are not merely allowed to rejoice, but authoritatively commanded, and if we do not we are guilty of disobedience.'

'But do you always rejoice?'

'Now this is a very common way of getting away from the authority of God, by comparing ourselves with one another instead of bowing to God's demands. Alas!

no, I do not rejoice always; but when I do not, I have to confess it as my sin, just as I have to confess every hour that I do not love God and my neighbour perfectly.'

'Many earnest men disobey this commandment of the Holy Ghost, I am sure, because they feel the evil of their own hearts so strongly.'

'Now this is most absurd from a scriptural point of view. In fact, the very step on which a Christian plants his foot, and thence rises to true joy and true worship, is the total setting aside of his own evil nature, as so utterly worthless, unimprovable, and corrupt, that he determines, by God's help, he will have no confidence in it. If a man gets thoroughly into this scriptural truth about "the flesh," or rather, if it enters into him by the power of the Holy Ghost, he will soon rise into the higher experience of rejoicing in Christ Jesus, and then worshipping God in the Spirit.

'We shall try briefly to note the Scriptures that give us the history, character, and relations of this terrible foe, and from Scripture we shall find that man as man is no better and no worse that when he was driven out of Eden. Science and art have done much. Printing, railways, telegraphs, and many other inventions have appeared. Time and space, as to this little planet, have been almost annihilated. But what about real progress Godward? With all man's so-called improvements, are there fewer thieves? Has honesty risen much above the level of policy? Are servants more obedient to their masters? Are children more obedient to their parents? Development has been going on; but, alas! what a development! The elements of all that has been developed were in Adam after the fall. Before the fall, Adam in innocence had body, soul, and spirit, with a will subject to God's will. By the fall he got the fatal acquisition, "the flesh,"—a self-will—a will independent of God's.'

Astronomers tell us that planets are kept in their courses by two forces acting in different directions, the resultant of which is the curve they describe round the sun. The one of these forces would draw the planet *from* the sun, the other would draw the planet to the sun. The one force is centrifugal, the other is centripetal. Man, revolving around God in the communion of innocence, having received the breath of life from God, making him immortal, and having been made in the image of God, acted as the representative of God on earth below. By the fall he severed his centripetal connection, or that which made him seek God, so that his action when he heard God's voice was to hide himself He has now acquired this fatal self-will. He has got the power to disobey God. The fatal freedom is his that some planet let loose from its circular path would have; and now, in his mad, desolating, destructive, rebellious, God-dishonouring freedom, man, as man, is rushing on to everlasting chaos, confusion, and night, ' the blackness of darkness for ever.' The least thing could sever the link that joined man in probation to God. Disobedience to one test-act did it. Man died (became separated from God) the moment he ate the forbidden fruit. What has been tie history of the world ever since?

Our modern sages tell us that it has been the education of the world, that at Babel men were divided into classes, that under law man's education begin in earnest, that Christ came as one of this great series of teachers, and now the Spirit in our day is going on to complete the education. This sounds very well, but it is only man's thought. Scripture shows us that the history of the world is the history of sin; 'that man is away from God and must be (not educated, but) saved or perish forever. The ritualist tells us that man is to be *Religionised;* God tells us that he is to be *born again*. The rationalist tells us he has been going on with his *education*; God tells us he is '*condemned* already,' and is incapable of being educated until His grace save him (Tit. ii.).

We have seen whence 'the flesh' was acquired: let us look at it—

I. As Tried and Described by God.

There are two distinct though connected questions:

First, What is the history of 'the flesh?'

Second, How is 'the flesh' described in Scripture?

I may state here, that there is often confusion in men's minds concerning what 'the flesh' is. This partly arises from the word 'flesh' being used in two quite different senses in Scripture. In the majority of cases in the New Testament the words rightly translated ' flesh ' and ' fleshly,' have to do with the flesh of the body, such as ' flesh and blood,' 'Jesus Christ came in the flesh,' which of course is not the evil nature which is spoken of in the other use of the word. There was an old heresy which made sin resident in the flesh of the body, and this led men to practise tortures and penance; but very few ever have' such a thought now. There are about a hundred passages in which ' flesh ' has this first meaning. In the fifty others in which the word is used it refers to the evil nature, the alienated affections, the self-will of man as away from God.

First, *What is the history of the flesh?*

A solution of arsenic in a glass full of water is very like the water, and cannot be detected by the eye. The chemist, in order to prove to the satisfaction of all that it is the deadly poison, takes one portion and to it adds something else, which, whenever it comes in contact with this arsenic in the water, makes it assume a well-known colour, showing at once what it is. lie then takes another quantity and adds something else to it to confirm this, until by various tests he has shown us exactly what it is, and proved beyond a doubt that it is that poison. God has been doing this with man; not, as the rationalist would persuade us, trying to improve the arsenic, and make it a harmless drink—arsenic remains arsenic. A farmer, having a hundred acres of land, when trying certain manures and crops, does not require to put all the land under one trial, but may have a hundred distinct trials on his hundred acres. God did not try man twice in innocence. He did not put two nations under law. Man is man, all as to nature being of the same material. Let us look at some of these tests that God has been employing from age to age.

1st, As an innocent man, God gave him one test — a thing which in itself had no moral value. He was allowed all the fruit in the garden except that upon one tree. The simplicity of the test made it all the more important. Man chose his own way' showed his independence, that is to say, sin as to his will. God knew what was in man. It was not for Himself He tried man. He knew the end from the beginning; but that all might know it, and every mouth be stopped, man was tested.

2d, After the fall man was tried as having a will opposed to God, and a conscience that told of God's demands. Man had the knowledge now of good and evil. His conscience told him what he *ought* to do; he had no external laws to obey. 'Leave a man to his conscience,' we hear it said. We answer, 'He has been left,' and what do we see? That as the one test acting on innocent man brought out his independence or sin as to the will, so man, with the flesh in him left to conscience, manifested his corruption or depravity of heart in lust, or sin as to the affections; for we read, 'God saw that the wickedness of man was great in the earth, and that every imagination (purposes and desires) of the thoughts of his heart was only evil continually.' Look at these three words, *'every,'* that is without exception, not one good, rotten to the core; *'only'* unadulterated evil, unmixed sinfulness; *'continually,'* at every moment, in so called good moments as well as bad. What a picture man, when he was left to his conscience, thus presented! God alone saw man's heart in its innate hideousness; and so, after man had been thus tested for nearly two thousand years, till sin reached its height, God destroyed all the teeming millions, in His wrath emptied out into destruction the earth odious in His presence, as a chemist hastens to throw out some noxious compound made between a poison and a test. We find God covenanting with Noah, and giving His promise to Abraham, and His *law* to Moses. This brings us to the third test.

3d, The law — the perfect rule of human righteousness, given to one nation, as the test was before given to one man, and conscience had tried all the world (the whole Gentile world being proved guilty by conscience and the light of nature, as seen in Rom. i.). What did the law do? Did it bring the nation to God? Here is what the Holy Ghost says, 'Wherefore then serveth the law? It was added *for the sake of (lit.)* transgression' (Gal. iii. 19). What was independence, that is, sin of the will or corruption — that is, sin of lust before — was now seen to be transgression — that is to say, sin in relation to law. ' Where no law is, there is no transgression,' We know, very well, there was sin — so much that the whole world had to be drowned; but law-showed sin to be transgression. A test, before it is of any use, must be perfect. If the test is imperfect, the results will prove nothing; but ' God's law is perfect,' it is 'holy, and just, and good;' and the moment it came in contact with 'the flesh' — with sinful man — it brought out his character as radically disobedient. Making the golden calf, and thus, breaking the first words of the law, was man's reception of the law. The law was weak to make sinful men holy, not in itself, but weak through the flesh. Fouler and fouler the filthy water of the flesh is shown to be. Can anything be worse than independence (away from God), corruption, and transgression? Yes, one thing more was needed before the trial of the flesh could be completed. Passing over man's declension under kings subject to God, and Gentile wickedness in unlimited monarchy over the whole world, we come to Christ as the last test at the 'end of the world' under trial.

4th, Christ is seen as a test of men. A servant might be very independent, or very corrupt, or break his master's commands, but he might never, with all this, have thought of taking his master's life. If the testing process had stopped short of Christ as a test, the nature of the flesh would not have been fully seen; but He has proved what man is. We are so much accustomed to think of Christ as a Saviour, that we seldom think of Him as coming to bring out ' what was in man.' Read Mark xii. 1-10. After showing man in his treatment of subordinate servants, the Lord says, ver. 6, ' Having yet, therefore, one Son, His well-beloved. He sent Him also last unto them saying, "They will reverence My Son."' We know well what they did: they slew the King's Son, showing thus their enmity to the King. Enmity against God Himself is the highest point rebellion can reach. This was never seen till Christ came; and this is the education of the world! Let us recapitulate what we have seen to be the character of man from his history. God tested him, and the very first thing recorded under each test is evil.

1st, As tried in innocence, his *independence* was seen — that is, sin as to the will.

2nd, As tried by conscience, his *corruption* was seen — that is, sin as to the heart.

3rd, As tried by law, his *transgression* was seen — that is, sin as to commandment.

4th, As tried by Christ, his *enmity* was seen — that is, sin as to a person.

The complete character of the poison is now seen — the flesh 'would kill God if it could. Man in the 'flesh' slaughtered the God-man. Friend, you have that nature in your bosom.

Second, *How is the flesh described?*

How does God describe it in the doctrinal statements of His word? It is remarkable that it is not until the full proof had been given of what the flesh can do — namely, crucify Christ—that we get it spoken of and fully exposed by God, and from God get its true character. The flesh as not borne with now on account of the hardness of men's hearts, but the darkness is past, and the true light now shineth. In Rom. vii. 18, Paul says, 'I know that in me (that is, in my Flesh) dwelleth no good thing.' This proves the existence of two natures in the Christian as well as the fearfully depraved character of the flesh. The Holy Ghost dwelt in the new nature in Paul as He dwells in every Christian. But besides his new nature there was still the old, unchanged and unchangeable. None but a saved man can know that there is *nothing good* whatever in the 'flesh.' Many moral unconverted men believe that there are many bad things in it, but none of them believe that there is nothing good. 'Even the worst have their good points' is man's estimate (and quite true as to human morality); but God's estimate is 'nothing good.' Read Gen. vi 5. All confess they are sinners, but few that they (as sprung from Adam) are nothing but sinners. The extent of the ruin, the nature of the depravity, and the steps by which it was reached, are of comparatively little importance, since in every unconverted man (as God sees him) there is no good thing.

A friend who had been led to see this, thus wrote to me, 'I have labelled all *my* feelings with God's label, "No good thing."' When very bad characters get converted, their friends often say, 'But you see he was a thoughtless young man, and he was led away, but he was not so bad as some;' and so on with a great deal of palliation and whining sentimentalism, instead of affixing to him God's estimate of every unconverted man, 'No good thing.'

Some people think, because they understand a great deal of theological truth, that this is good. Unless the man has been born again, all his knowledge however good in itself is reckoned ' no good thing' to him.

Some think that because they feel devotional amid solemn sights and plaintive pealing pipes of praising machinery, there must be some soft corner for divine things in their hearts after all, but God all the while says, '*No good thing.*' Hearing the 'Dead March in Saul' played by a military band at a soldier's funeral has often moved many to tears, and I do not wonder at the most stolid being moved in their feelings; but what does mere feeling or emotion amount to? — '*No good thing.'*

Some again suppose because their consciences get disturbed at certain sins, that this is so much good. Man has nothing to boast of in having a conscience, not even if he followed its right leadings. It never gave him a new nature. Every man has a conscience, that is to say—the knowledge of good and evil. A man cannot make a warm day because he has a thermometer which shows when it is warm. Neither has a man anything good, because he has within him that which tells him what is good, and what is evil. Let us look at other Scriptures to find out a little more what the flesh is.

Gal. v. 19, 'The works of *the flesh* are manifest, which are, adultery, fornication, uncleanness, lasciviousness, idolatry, witchcraft, hatred, variance, emulations, wrath, strife, seditions, heresies, envyings, murders, drunkenness, revellings, and such like.' What a fountain of all uncleanness! In 2 Pet. ii. 18 we find what feeds the flesh: ' For when they speak great swelling words of vanity, they allure through the lusts of *the flesh*.'' The flesh loves pompousness, it hates humility. 2 Pet. ii. 10 speaks of 'them that walk after the flesh in the lust of uncleanness, and despise government — presumptuous, self-willed.' ' Self-will' (that is, liking and choosing one's own way rather than God's), ' is, in fact, the very essence of the flesh.' Man must have what he wills, and desires, whatever the consequences be, whatever God says; Satan, of course, at the same time blinding us as to what God's will is. The world is also in close alliance with its lusts: i John ii. 16, ' All that is in the world, the lust of *the flesh*, and the lust of the eyes, and the pride of life, is not of the Father, but is of the world.'

Rom. viii. 3-7 gives us the nature of the flesh as opposed to *law*, to *life*, and to *God*, just as we saw it in its progressive history. Ver. 3, ' What the law could not do in that it was weak through the flesh;' ver. 7, 'The carnal mind (literally the mind of *the flesh*) is not subject to the *law* of God, neither indeed can be.' It opposed the law, broke it, was stirred up to more evil by it. Again, as to life: ver. 6, 'To be carnally minded (literally the mind of *the flesh*) is death;' and as to God, 'The *carnal* mind is *enmity* against God;' ver. 8, 'So then they that are in *the flesh* cannot please God.' Friend, pause a minute. Are you in the flesh? Do what you may, you 'cannot please God.' Give all your time and money to the Lord, yet you ' cannot please God.' Let us now look at ' the flesh' —

II. As to the Sinner's Salvation.

We need not dwell long on this, as we have seen what God's character of it is. 'The flesh' is never sanctified nor improved. It can only be condemned.

Christ came in the likeness of sinful flesh, and for sin condemned ' sin in *the flesh*.' 'The flesh' is never forgiven. It is judged, set aside, condemned. Though my sins were like scarlet, the precious blood has cleansed them, and I am forgiven, but the flesh never is. God never improves it, and God never forgives it, neither should we. We are saved from this awful depravity and corruption in which we were born, not by any process or work, any more than we are justified from our sins by a work.

We get out of *the flesh* just as we got into it. We got into it by our birth; we get out of it by a new birth. We got into it in a representative head, Adam; we get out of it in the representative head, Christ. Christ on the cross not only had our iniquities 'laid upon Him, but also condemned ' sin in *the flesh*; ' that is to say, not the guilt of sin,

88

but sin in the nature; not the branches, but the root; not the streams, but the fountain.

Many are trying to improve 'the flesh,' and would take much comfort if they could only feel themselves getting a little better; whereas God wishes us to have no confidence in it whatever, and to ' reckon ourselves dead indeed *unto sin.*How could anyone by any effort of will, without a new nature, subdue his flesh when it is just self-will? It would only be will against will, which is an absurdity.

But if I receive God's Christ as the One dead and now risen, reckoning myself dead to sin, I bring in God's will done in Christ's work about sin, and I thus 'thank God through Jesus Christ our Lord,' and begin to walk in newness of life. And though there is still conflict, I know that 'with the mind I myself (what God reckons as me in Christ) serve the law of God, but with the flesh the law of sin;' but that 'there is no condemnation to them in Christ Jesus.' Whether are you in Christ Jesus or in the flesh? You cannot be in both.

Your standing is either in Christ risen or in Adam fallen. There is no third man. Adam was the first man, and all the trial was only of the first man. Christ is the second man, and there is no third. He is the last. He is the second man, but he is the last Adam (i Cor. xv. 45, 49).

III. As to the Christian's Life

New Testament Scripture is very plain on two points:

1st. The Christian is not in *the flesh*. Paul could speak of himself and of all Christians thus, 'When we were in the flesh' (Rom. vii. 5), of course thus implying that they are not in it now.

2d. '*The flesh'* is still in the Christian. Paul said, 'In me, that is in my flesh, dwelleth no good thing.' (Rom. vii. 18.) If we mistake or forget one or other of these facts, we shall get into great confusion, and shall have lessened power in dealing with this enemy.

1st. The Christian Is Not in The Flesh.

'Ye are *not* in the flesh but in the Spirit, if so be that the Spirit of God dwell in you.' (Rom. viii. 9.) The Spirit of God dwells in all Christians, therefore this is true of all. 'They that are Christ's *have crucified* the flesh with the afflictions and lusts.' (Gal. v. 24.) Not, ' are to crucify,' or ' ought to,' but ' have crucified.' ' In whom also ye are circumcised with the circumcision made without hands, in putting off the body of the sins of *the flesh* by the circumcision of Christ.' (Col. ii. II.) Every Christian is out of Adam and in Christ. He is sailing now in the river of life; whereas, by nature, his boat is tossing on the river of death. It is said of the children of Israel in the wilderness, so wicked and so perverse, God 'hath not beheld iniquity in Jacob, neither hath He seen perverseness in Israel.' (Num. xxiii. 21.) So when God looks at a sinner in Christ he sees the sinner dressed in all the beauty of Christ and sees none of the sinner's iniquity nor perverseness.

The Holy Spirit, by the pen of the Apostle Paul, brings out this very clearly in the second chapter of Galatians, where a line of argument is pursued similar to that contained in the sixth of Romans. In Romans, after Paul brings in ' all the world,' Jew and Gentile, 'guilty before God,' and demonstrates the victory of grace over sin, he goes on in the sixth chapter to shew Christ, in resurrection, as the immediate and effective power of personal holiness.

In the second of Galatian she takes occasion, from Peter refusing to take a meal with certain persons, to shew the true position and standing of all believers in the Lord Jesus Christ. A straw shews the direction of the current. If Peter could not have intercourse with Gentiles who had been cleansed in the blood of Jesus and placed in a position of righteousness that no legal observances could effort or help him to keep and walk in, the whole 'gospel of the grace of God would be undermined. (Read Gal. ii.)

Paul shews that both Peter and himself, Jews as they were, children of the promise, and not 'sinners of the Gentiles,' had to fall into the sinner's place, and accept Christ the gift of God.

Peter, in Acts xv. ii, stands up for the very same doctrine: — 'We believe that, through the grace of the Lord Jesus Christ, we (Jews) shall be saved, even as they (sinners of the Gentiles).'

Paul says, in effect, if the law could justify them, they had been doing wrong in preaching Christ. Does Christ need the law to help Him to present the believer to God? We consider it blasphemous to think that Christ would be a minister of sin. But having been judged, condemned, and slain by the law, do we now go back to be saved or helped by it? If so, we prove by this very act that we are 'transgressors;' for in that case we should never have left it at all. Grace and law cannot help each other in our salvation—the adoption of grace is the giving up of law for salvation.

The Apostle, in the 18th and following verses (Gal. ii.) places himself as representing all believers, and goes on to show that men can serve God, and live acceptably to Him—only through death and resurrection. 'For I through the law am dead.' This, of course, cannot mean that I am morally dead to the knowledge of its demands; nor that I am dead in the sense of seeking my justification by the old dispensation under law; but ' I *through* the law have died,' or have judicially met my doom. God said, 'In the day that thou eatest thereof thou shalt surely die.' The flaming sword that guarded Paradise has demanded my blood. 'I have died.' 'The soul that sinneth it shall die.' 'I have died.' The law has exacted its demands. 'The wages of sin is death.' These wages have been paid 'I have died.'

But, since I through the law have died, in perfect righteousness and justice I have now died to its every claim, and the sword cannot be bathed in blood twice for the same offence. The wages of my sin cannot be demanded twice. The murderer hanging dead at the jibbet of justice is dead to every demand they can bring against him.

Daniel, by serving his God, had brought himself under the penalty of the laws of the Medes and Persians, which said, 'He shall be cast into the den of lions.' But, sitting at the bottom of that den, with the lions' mouths graciously stopped, he could say, — 'I am dead *to* the law of the Medes and Persians.' And when Darius raised him on the morrow, he did so in perfect righteousness, as far as the demands of the law of the Medes and Persians were concerned, and no enemy of Daniel, no adviser of Darius, could punish the prophet for law-breaking, nor point a suspicious finger at him as he sat with Darius — he could now live to Darius. 'I through the law am dead to the law,' only, however, ' that I might live unto God.' — 'He that has died is justified from sin' (Rom. vi. 7). This death and resurrection scheme is no figure of speech, but an awful reality as seen at Calvary, and a reality (judicially and experimentally) to the sinner on believing in Jesus. We have life out of death.

The 19th verse is a counterpart of the i8th. The 18th, as it were, expresses the truth abstractly. The 19th meets this question, — 'What! is Saul the Pharisee, Saul the persecutor, Saul the professor, Saul the legalist, dead?' He is; but this is where I find an end of myself—on the cross of Christ: ' I am crucified with Christ.' This is sometimes explained, ' as Christ was crucified, and suffered at the hands of the world, so I'll bear the cross along with Him.' It is indeed a blessed truth that we have fellowship with Him in His sufferings for righteousness, and that as followers of Jesus, we are to take up *our* cross and follow Him: but the truth in this passage answers to the statement in the former verse, 'I through the law have died;' and to that in Romans vi. 6, ' Knowing that our old man is (has been) crucified.' 'I have been crucified with Christ' (The verb is in the perfect passive). The stroke of justice against me fell on Him. My cup was drained by Him; my wages of sin were paid out to Him; my separation from God was in His cry, 'My God, my God, why hast thou forsaken me?' My hell was borne by Him — the perfectly righteous One fulfilling all law, and then bearing its penalty for me the unrighteous, condemned, dead one. ' He suffered, the Just for the unjust, that He might bring us to God.' And, looking back on His cross, and identifying myself with Him, I can say,—

'I through the law am dead,'
'I am crucified with Christ.'

No demand can be made against Christ; for, after justice had been appeased, God raised Him up from the dead by the Holy Spirit; and as there could never come one single question concerning sin against Him who had become the sin-bearer (after having borne sin. He had been raised in righteousness), so I, quickened into this 'newness of life,' go free. I was not justified when Christ rose, but He was raised again for my justification; and on believing I reckon myself dead, and can say,—

I am dead to the law,'
'Crucified; nevertheless I live,'

live in this resurrection-life, live in this life that Jesus has beyond his grave, beyond the demands of law, beyond the doom of sin, for it is 'yet not literally no longer I, but Christ liveth in me'— no longer Saul the Pharisee—Saul the pretender to—and striver after, righteousness by law' but one who has submitted himself to God's righteousness—one who has submitted himself to be put out of existence judicially—that is to say, in God's reckoning—and is now known only as one who is living in Christ, living unto God,—

'That I might live unto God;'
'Yet not I, but Christ liveth in me.'

A man is thus made fit for living unto God, not by amendment and reformation, but through *death* and *resurrection*,' the flesh might and does attempt the former, in the latter God alone can work. This 'sanctification of the spirit' is all of God.

'The *life* which I now live,' is in a foreign, uncongenial clime—where I have no friends—no food—no rest; it lives by faith,' on what will be its life for ever, 'the Son of God.' This life feeds on love: for its object is Jesus, 'who loved me and gave Himself for me.

Thus I have not only forgiveness of sins in Christ, but righteousness also; for I could no more get righteousness by law, than I could forgiveness. But now are we 'the righteousness of God in Him.' 'For if righteousness come bylaw, Christ is dead in vain;' but we are in Him 'who of God is made unto us wisdom, and righteousness, and sanctification, and redemption' (i Cor. i. 30).

> 'With Christ we died to sin —
>   Lay buried in His tomb;
> But quickened now with Him our life,
>   We stand beyond our doom.'

Thus the apostle Paul places the believer in perfect acceptance before God — Christ his title — Christ his righteousness — Christ his meetness — Christ his all and in all. Made a 'partaker of the divine nature,' the believer has now that which can enjoy God, and commune with Him.

But what has all this truth to do with the Christian's every-day life, one may ask? Much, very much indeed; for there can be no real progress made by us in the Christian course until the ground of our standing before God be righteously and conclusively settled.

Being born of Adam, 'of the will of the flesh,' we are heirs of Adam's nature, its guilt, its actings, and its doom, ' by nature the children of wrath.' So having received Christ, 'being born of God,' we are reckoned as one with Christ, we were crucified with Christ, and thus met the doom of sin in Christ: and now we live to God in the life of. Christ, a life in resurrection, as truly getting a new nature at the second birth, as we got the Adam-nature at the first. God reckons us as being thus in His sight; and we believing, and thus getting into God's reckoning, have 'peace with God, through our Lord Jesus Christ.'

No Christian ever lived, or ever will live, on earth without sin in him. Indeed it is after I know Christ that I really know the utter worthlessness of the flesh, that 'in me (that is in my flesh) *dwelleth* no good thing' (Rom. vii. 18). Now the opposition will be felt between this perfectly holy nature, begotten in me in connexion with Christ risen and gone to the Father, and this perfectly sinful nature. Now it is that I know the meaning of 'sin that dwelleth in me,' which can never be uprooted here, for it dwelleth in me; not sins coming from me, or felt by me, but sin, the innate principle, no accident nor habit,' sin dwelleth in me.' Formerly I might have assumed that the doctrine of *in-dwelling sin* was true, but now 'I know' (Rom. vii. i8), that is, the truth is applied to my conscience, by the Holy Ghost. Now I know, ' that the disposition of the flesh (*lit.*) is enmity against God, for it is not subject to the law of God, *neither indeed can be* (Rom. viii. 7).

From the above it will be seen that salvation is something more than a mere payment of debt, a covering over of iniquity, the gift of a white robe of righteousness, a setting right of the faculties of the soul, for which out of gratitude to God, and aided by His Spirit, the Christian is now to live a holy life. There is also a new birth, the

implantation of a nature which not only makes a man live to serve God out of gratitude, but which in its very essence is from God. The spring of all true Christian holiness is the presence and operative power of the indwelling Spirit, working indeed
through a man's natural faculties, but on objects above and beyond what the Adam-
life can see, apprehend, live on, or enjoy. Three very important and practical propo-
sitions arise out of the foregoing truths.

1st, The Christian has two natures in one person.
2d, How does the Christian grow in grace?
3d, The Christian daily confesses his sins and is daily forgiven.

I. The Christian has two district natures in one responsible person.

The Christian is not two persons, the one perfectly sinful, and the other perfectly
sinless, shut up together in one chamber; but he has two natures, the 'old' and the
'new man' in the one responsible person; he has that born of the flesh, which is not
merely flesh-like but *flesh*, and that born of the Spirit, which is not merely spiritual
but *spirit.*

The sinner living '*in the flesh*,' Mead in trespasses and sins, was pardoned, accepted, and made a saint — Christ having died and risen for him, by being born again,
which was accomplished by getting this life of Christ, begotten in him by the Holy
Ghost in reality and not in figure. As a saint, he is, now 'not in the flesh,' though the
flesh is in him, but he is in the Spirit, and is responsible for the uprisings and sins of
the old man. He is henceforth pardoned as a son according to the value of the blood
presented before God *for him*, the person, the individual now become a Christian,
the man possessed of these two natures, who should be walking 'in the spirit,'
though ever and anon he is made to stumble through the power of the flesh' Thus
the saint does not advance in sanctification by a change being effected in the character of either nature, but in the gradual development of ' the new man ' by means of
the inworking of the Holy Ghost, and in the daily mortification of the members
which are upon the earth. The man is thus gradually sanctified and made more like
Jesus. This is growth 'in grace.' How blessed! We are saved 'by *grace*;' we stand 'in
grace' — we grow '*in grace*'. The life of a child is perfectly human; we have to grow
to be men. The smallest leaflet on the furthest branch of the vine has the same vine-
life as the largest branch, the trunk or the root. God's-seed implanted is a perfect
life: we have to grow up to the stature of men. We would again sum up, in brief, regarding this new life which we have already discoursed on at length in the chapter
on the work of the Spirit.

In John iii. we get the origin and communication of this life, 'Ye must be born
again' (ver. 7): something external, all of God, must be implanted; not something
already in me wrought on and purified. 'Of water and of the Spirit:' the word of God
applied by the Spirit purifies us as to our thoughts, feelings, and afflictions.

In John iv. we get the indwelling of the Spirit — the gift of Christ — as the on'"
energizing power in the new man, represented as 'a well of water springing up into
everlasting life' (iv. 14). In chap. vii. we get the outflow of this Spirit, in the activities
of the new man on all around him, through no new channels, no new faculties of
mind, but ' out of his belly shall flow rivers of living water' (ver. 38).

2. How does the Christian grow in grace? Does his old heart get better?

The Spirit of God in John teaches that in a converted man there is a new fountain.

Many Christians seem to think that all we get at conversion is a divinely given *filter* to the old fountain, which will gradually increase in its power until it renders the filthy waters of the old fountain clean. In Galatians v. 15-26, the whole point is stated. Two *fountains* are spoken of in the converted man, sending out their natural streams. The streams from the old fountain, the flesh, are given at the 19th verse, ' Adultery, fornication, uncleanness, lasciviousness, idolatry, witchcraft, hatred, variance, emulations, wrath, strife, seditions, heresies, envyings, murders, drunkenness, revellings. Are we anywhere taught in Scripture that this evil nature is refined, is purified? Certainly, indeed, the man, the individual, is purified, is cleansed, made more holy, is morally sanctified; but it is in altogether another way than by trying to cure what is ' incurably wicked.' The streams from the new fountain — the Spirit — are given at the 22d verse,' love, joy, peace, long-suffering, gentleness, goodness, faith, meekness, temperance; ' arc) we are told that the Christian's holy life is walking in the Spirit, mortifying the 'members which arc upon the earth' (Col. iii. 5), keeping them in their place of death, ' not fulfilling the lusts of the flesh.' This is God's way; He asks for a holy walk, and moreover has not left us powerless, as helpless slaves under the flesh, but has placed us in a position above it, as masters over it — for 'the flesh lusteth against the Spirit,' also the ' Spirit against the flesh, and these are contrary the one to the other' (therefore they can never be merged the one into the other, nor come to peaceable terms) *'in order that'* (literally) ye may not do the things that ye would.' Not, as generally understood, that I should wish to do good things but cannot (we get that aspect of truth in the case of a quickened man under law in Rom. vii. 19, but it is another thought here); on the contrary, by the flesh-nature I wish to do evil things, but now I have the Spirit indwelling and acting, who will not let me do those evil things I otherwise would.

Many Christians do not know that we get a new creation put into us at the new birth: hence they do not realise the existence in the believer of two diametrically opposite and actively opposing natures. Ignorance of these things is at the root of many soul-confounding errors in doctrine and practice.

If salvation consisted merely in having forgiveness, the powers of the mind being set right, and the will wrought on and sanctified, we might be saved to-day and lost to-morrow; in Christ to-day and out of Him to-morrow. But if I get a divine life — the child's life ' quickened together with Christ,' united to Christ by the Holy Ghost sent down from heaven — I am as eternally saved as Christ is safe, being a ' member of His body, of His flesh, and of His bones' (Eph. v. 30).

Again, if my sinful propensities have merely to be toned down, so that they gradually die out, one by one, until all of them are out of existence; if I were to live long enough, and were sufficiently zealous, watchful, and pra3'erful, I might obtain perfection as to holiness, in this moral sense, — might live without having sin at all. This we know is opposed to all Scripture teaching, for (it is written of Christians) ' If we say that we have no sin, we deceive ourselves, and the truth is not in us.' It is equally opposed to all conscientious Christian experience, for while we *ought* at all times to walk 'in the Spirit' without sinning, we know that the unchanged and unchangeable root of sin remains till we go hence. That kind of teaching which speaks of the attainment of perfection in the walk of a Christian — that is to say, the possibility of sinless perfection, perfect sanctification in the flesh, tends miserably to tone down sin, and make it a slight matter, and sacrilegiously brings down God's standard of holiness to human attainment, instead of having all in Christ: Christ *for me* — my Substitute: Christ *in me* — my life.

In I John iii. 9, we read, ' Whosoever is born of God doth not commit sin; for His seed remaineth in him, and he cannot sin, because he is born of God.' Mark very carefully that this is not written concerning a few advanced Christians who had reached a high state of perfection. It is written concerning the youngest disciple: 'Whosoever is born of God.' And would it not be strange to think that anything born of God could sin? The difficulty in the passage vanishes when I understand that the Christian has two natures, one born of God, perfect and sinless (God's seed is in him), the other born of Adam, imperfect and sinful. Whenever a Christian commits a sin, he is not manifesting that he is born of God, but is shewing that he is born of Adam. It is not as. born of God he sins, but as born of Adam. Should we not watch over ourselves, and pray for much grace, to enable us always to live as sons of God, and not as sons of Adam.''

It is Christians who are told, in Phil. iii. 3, to have no 'confidence in the flesh.' Those who are the true circumcision of God have no confidence in any religious culture, advantages, or natural privileges. Paul could boast more than any man of natural trainings for the flesh. Born under and brought up in all God's ordinances, he yet had to renounce all. God's ordinance can never implant life. All our many privileges could never implant the new life. They can, and do develop the life, as the heat, sunshine, rain, and culture do a seed; but an act of God's Spirit is required to implant the seed. These same privileges may only the more surely seal the ruin of a man who has not been converted, and it may be impossible to renew him to repentance. The sun hardens clay as it softens wax. Paul thought all his natural advantages but loss. He had no confidence in the flesh. Two are striving for the mastery in every Christian, the flesh and the spirit — 'for the flesh lusts against the Spirit, and the Spirit against the flesh.' But we have now the upper hand, and sin shall not have dominion over us. It dwells in us, but shall not reign over us. It is by opposition and warfare, not by assimilation and agreement, that we grow in the Christian life. We are not daily sanctified by the 'flesh' getting better or less, but by the new nature in us growing and being strengthened by the indwelling Spirit of God, and thus successfully opposing the first risings of the flesh. We cannot expel the flesh — we reckon it dead, put it off, and keep it under. We mortify our members which are upon the earth. We cannot root out the vile weeds — we keep the scythe going cutting them down.

All Christians would wish to be led by the Spirit: but they forget the first step, to start with a vote of '*no confidence*' in the flesh. At every subsequent step there will then be watchfulness as well as looking to Jesus, who is our strength. The Christian has not so much to fear ' the flesh' in its outwardly gross forms, as in its thoughts and desires. It is comparatively easy not to steal, not to tell lies, not to swear, not to be a drunkard.

Many moral, unconverted men are specimens of the highest external right-doing, but it is in its secret workings, workings that are natural to us, that we have the flesh most to dread.

Our path is that of obedience and love in the footsteps of our Lord, where the righteous requirements of the law are 'fulfilled in us, who walk not after *the flesh*, but after the Spirit' (Rom. viii. 4), for the flesh gave us nothing in the past, and can profit us nothing for the future: thus 'We are debtors not to the flesh, to live after the flesh.' For 'If ye live after the flesh, ye shall die; but if ye through the Spirit do mortify the deeds of the body, ye shall live' (Rom. viii. 12, 13). Our sonship cannot be taken from us, but we can have no living fellowship with God if we thus walk. 'Living after the flesh' and communion are impossible, and cannot go together. Death is separation from God — not 'ceasing to exist;' for we know that not even the lost thus perish. Death is ceasing to exist in one state or condition, and existing in another state separated from God.

Take care, fellow-disciple, of getting into a deadened state of soul. We have the flesh in us, yet we have no authority, but the reverse, for living after it, ' as if we walked according to the flesh' (2 Cor. x. 2). Stamp upon it 'No confidence' — 'Put ye on the Lord Jesus Christ, and make not provision for the flesh, to fulfil the lusts thereof' (Rom. xiii. 14). Alas! how often we make provision for it! How the flesh feasts upon praise and flattery! It likes to be flattered, and when it is not flattered, it begins to flatter. It understands nothing about being of ' no reputation.' It likes to be something, or to do something.

'Though I be nothing' is not in its vocabulary. Have I done something for the Lord? Have I been the poor, humble channel to convey water to a soul? The flesh likes to know it. 'Let not thy left hand know what thy right hand doeth' — is God's way. ' Let not only your left hand, but let every person know' — is man's way. 'I did so and so. I was used in so and so.' Oh, this fearful self! This awful I! And then it, of course, vindicates itself. ' Oh, but it is for God's glory that I tell it! ' Yes; this may be the worst part of the whole —taking a little to self under semblance of giving all to God. ' No provision,' 'no confidence' in your own evil nature, or any other person's. Take care of being 'vainly puffed up' by the mind of the flesh (Col. ii. i8). Do not be unkind to a fellow-believer by bringing near him that which the flesh enjoys. Do not bring sparks near gunpowder. 'Oh, you did well to-day!' said one to another who had preached the gospel. ' Yes,' he replied, 'Satan told me that before I left the pulpit.' Let us not serve Satan after this sort.

None are in greater danger than those who are used to gather in souls. I knew one who was constantly used of God in doing all kinds of good, and when he did speak, it was always about what other people had been doing. To tell faults to a friend himself is faithfulness. All that is good of him tell to others. God tells us of our faults. He stands up for us against every accuser. Another I knew who could speak of what self had been used in doing, but could not bear to hear of others being used. What a God-dishonouring, flesh-gratifying as well as foolish course! Are we not members one of another? I heard it said of a dear Christian one day, 'Yes, such a one lives upon praise.' Do you live upon the rejected Lord, who made Himself of no reputation, or on praise? Husks that the swine live upon! Make no provision for the flesh.

'Having, therefore, these promises (the Lord Almighty to be our Father), dearly beloved, let us cleanse ourselves from all filthiness of *the flesh* and spirit, perfecting holiness in the fear of God.' (2 Cor. vii. i.) You cannot be growing in grace, advancing in holiness, in these providings for the flesh. While the grace of God is not to be dimmed for a moment, let us remember that we are under the righteous government of our Father, and 'he that soweth to his flesh shall of the flesh reap corruption.' Christians suffer, and suffer sadly, by sowing to or making provision for the flesh. Our only safeguard is Christ. With our eye steadfastly and constantly fixed on Him — following Him, copying Him, tilled with Him — we shall be led into holiness of life, and neither into licentiousness nor into legalism. For while at the one extreme we may be led into licentiousness or carelessness of walk by our subtle foes, we may meet another danger, which is asceticism and penance, a dishonour to the body by coming under worldly ordnances (such as touch not, taste not, handle not), which look very like holiness and consecration to God neglecting our bodies, but the only effect is that they tend 'to the satisfying of the flesh.' (Col. ii. 20.) For it feasts on whatever is against Christ, and is satisfied with whatever takes the eye from Him.

'But will not the Holy Spirit keep his own from all this?' I have been asked. 'Yes; but the way He does keep us from the power of the flesh is by enabling us to give it no food, no provision, no satisfaction.' Whatever feeds the spirit starves the flesh. So the apostle Peter by the Holy Ghost says, 'Dearly beloved, I beseech you, as strangers and pilgrims, abstain from fleshly lusts, which war against the soul.' (i Pet. ii. 11.) The ways of men around are strange ways to us. They think these advices far above human reach (and so they are) but we are living the life of Christ; and as such, we are to hate, ' even the garment spotted by the flesh.' (Jude 23.) Alas! how little watching and praying there is among Christians — how little we live on Christ! If we lived with Him ever before us, ever filling us, our only satisfaction, our joy for ever, what power should we gain over 'the flesh!'

Christians learn what the 'flesh' is —

1st, By experience of its unmingled vileness before conversion; or of its horrid lusts and sad sins after conversion; or

2d, By taking God's character of it from His Word.

When God gives us His 'Memoirs of olden times,' He does not leave out the actings of the flesh. When the ' chronicles of the spirits of just men made perfect' pass before us in Heb. xi., their sins and iniquities are remembered no more. I have been much struck with the unreal life people are led into by reading memoirs of good people, where the good in their lives is told but not the evil; where the triumph is seen but not the conflict. It is just like 'novel literature,' that gives such unreal ideas to young people, and unfits them for everyday life. So most memoirs, by not bringing prominently forward the everyday conflicts, the evil foe within, often do more real harm than permanent good. Read God's own histories. Many human ones would do for angels or seraphs to read, but they are not for militant saints. ' Follow me,' says the Perfect One, and 'Jesus only,' is enough.

Dear worker-for-God, Met no man take thy crown. 'Take care of this foe. A brother in the Lord used to say often to himself, before going to do anything for God, as preaching, &c., 'Now, soul, honour bright, is this for the glory of God?' We need a great deal more of bright, sterling honour between God and our souls, and also between one another. We fear the flesh most from its gradual uprisings. It has begun to work often before we are aware, and not till some text meets us straight in the face do we discover that the flesh has been working. Again, our religionised and pious flesh is often a great snare; that is to say, we sometimes begin to think that a Christian's 'flesh' is better than an unconverted man's 'flesh;' but, if we do, we proceed on false grounds, and will reap nothing but failure. First look to Jesus away from your vile, unimproveable heart, live in the Spirit, and keep looking to Jesus until you see Him as He is, and then you shall be like Him, done with this evil heart, this corrupt nature, this self-willed flesh. Meantime we have to be daily, hourly confessing sin, and in this having the most blessed communion with God —'in light' that makes everything manifest, and overlooks nothing.

3. The Christian daily confesses his sins and is daily forgiven.

A perfect statement of the whole position, walk, and restoration of a Christian is found in i John i. If we are to have fellowship with the Father and the Son, we must have that life implanted in us by the Holy Ghost, that eternal, indestructible, perfect life, which is capable of having fellowship with God — that nature which throbs in harmony with God's nature, for we are 'partakers of the Divine nature.' (2 Pet. i. 4.)

'We are *not* sons.' Our place is now in the light and in the Spirit, and thus in communion; if we were walking in darkness, in unloving ways, it would be merely *saying* we have fellowship, and not the truth. God is now revealed as without a veil, and, wondrous truth! we saved sinners walk ' in the light as God is in the light'—in the exercise of that pure and perfect love (His perfect commandment) that this whole epistle is inculcating (i John ii. 9), following in the steps of Him who could say to the vilest confessed sinner, when accused by Pharisees, ' Neither do I condemn thee, go and sin no more.' He was '*the light of the world*' and becomes to all such as this sinner at His feet the *light of life*' (John viii. 12). Thus 'we have fellowship with one another,' because having communion and fellowship each with God. Here shall we be able to judge our own sins; in this very place, not when we get out of 'the light,' but 'in the light,' 'the blood of Jesus Christ his Son cleanseth *us* (believers, sons, those who have been born again) from all sin.' The blood is once applied and is of continued efficacy—not has cleansed or did cleanse but '*cleanseth* us from all sin.' The effect of light is not to make us believe or feel that we have no sin in us. Sin will be in every man, saint or sinner, till he goes hence; for ' If we say that we have no sin, we deceive ourselves and the truth is not in us.' And how am I to do with these sins that are still -uprising and which the light makes manifest, for the more light there is in a room the more the dust is seen? Listen to God's simple plan!

'If we confess our sins, He is faithful and just to forgive our sins, and to cleanse us from all unrighteousness.' Confess our *sins*, not our *sin*, not merely say, 'We are all sinners: God be merciful to me a sinner;' but judging the uprisings of the evil spring, according to God's standard of perfect holiness, which is Christ, confess all known sins, deeds, looks, thoughts. What heart-searching this implies! ' If we *confess* our sins,' not merely in words, we shall have a real individual dealing with our Father, not certainly as condemned sinners before an angry judge, but all the more close and real, because we are accepted sons dealing with such a holy, gracious Father.

' He is faithful and just.' It is no longer a matter of love and mercy, — *these* have indeed provided the way: but He is 'faithful,' for He hath said it, He is 'just,' on account of the blood presented there, 'to forgive,' and it is inexcusable unbelief not to 'confess,' confide, and believe that we are forgiven on the spot, and thus be ever walking in the light with a calm, holy joy.

The first two verses of the second chapter give the apostle's practical interpretation of these doctrines. 'My little children, these things write I unto you, that ye *sin not.*' No lower standard is set before us than absolutely '*sin not.*' 'Be ye holy, for I am holy' (i Pet. i. i6). Walk 'in the Spirit,' in the energy of the new life, and in the light; mortifying the deeds of the old man. This is certainly our aim, but in this we fail, aiming yet not attaining.

But 'if any man sin, we have an advocate' (a paraclete, literally),' with the Father, Jesus Christ *the Righteous*, and He is the propitiation for our sins; and not for ours only but also for the whole world.' That is to say, if any of us Christian., commit any sin as He sees sin, in His character of advocate He cleanses us from it. This is very blessed, for while we have to confess all known sin, and thus get it off our consciences, there are many sins which we do not see; but He has made Himself responsible to cleanse us from all sin which His holy eye sees. Our advocate does not say that we, His clients, are guilty and then plead for mercy. And He is a righteous advocate, therefore He can by no means clear the guilty, but, wondrous wisdom! wondrous truth! wondrous grace! He took our guilt upon Him, and now points to His own death as that which cleanses us from all sin. He sees the sin — He satisfies the Father—He is the advocate. He meets the accuser — He is the propitiation. What a perfect paraclete with the Father, ever keeping us clean by His blood before Him, as the paraclete, the Holy Ghost, whom He sent, is ever keeping us clean down here by the Word, washing the feet of those who are ' clean every whit' (John xiii.), removing from our consciences every thing that He sees would interrupt our fellowship and communion, by the word which He whispers to us (Eph. v. 26)

Believing Brother, —You have died and 'risen with Christ.' Is your affection set on those 'things which are above?' Do you think you have got into God's mind concerning your standing and acceptance? Blessed, most blessed, if you have! But does this lead you to be more holy, more Christ-like, more heavenly-minded, more anxious to walk in the way of God? If I, as a Christian, am ' not under the law ' (Rom. vi. 14), I am certainly under my Lord's commandments. 'If ye love Me keep my commandments' (John xiv. 15). 'For this is the love of God, that we keep His commandments; and His commandments are not grievous (i John v. 3). ' And this is His commandment, that we should believe on the name of His Son Jesus Christ, and ' (having believed — having the new life) 'love one another, as He gave us commandment' (i John iii. 23). If we read all the practical directions at the end of Romans, Ephesians, Colossians, &c., we shall find that Christians had to be again and again reminded whose they were, and how they ought to walk.

Two truths have to be kept in mind — the Christian is not under the law-principle — so much being exacted for so much — the taskmaster's w4iip held over his head, with its ' do-this-and-live ' demands — but is quickened into the life from God, in subjection to his Lord, 'enlawed to Christ' (i Cor. ix. 21): and walking in this wilderness, he is only too glad to get explicit directions concerning the minutiae of life, as well as its higher outlines; glad, amid confusion here, to know in what direction his Father's finger points, so that with all his soul he may judge his own sinful flesh, and walk whither his Father directs. Thus, in a very blessed way, the son delights in the law (the *torah*, literally ' finger-point') of his Father; he makes it his study, day and night. Are you loving to be guided by the eye of God along the platform of His eternal love, which is based on His infinite justice? Watch against a mere doctrinal or intellectual grasp of truth. Without the living powder 'knowledge puffeth up.' Beware of the pestilential swamps of a hateful antinomianism, that spirit of the flesh, so common all around in this day, and so apt to lurk in every heart. To whom much is given of him shod much be required. God has made you a son of such a Father-God, in that blessed, holy, separated walk, linked in eternal union with His own beloved Son. Shall we not walk like sons?

This reckoning of myself as crucified with Christ, put out of existence, as it were, in the crucifixion of Christ, and now identified with the living, risen Jesus, is not mysticism, but one of God's most important realities — foolishness, indeed, to the worldly-wise — a mystery, revealed by the Holy Ghost only to those who, self-emptied and helpless, listen as little children. When you believed in the Lord Jesus Christ did you not leave all your sins in the grave of Jesus (in God's reckoning)? Are they not sunk into the depths of the sea, to be remembered no more? Were you crucified with Christ? Then you have left the world also at Jesus' grave: the cross as truly stands between the Christian and 'the world,' as between the Christian and his sins. 'One with Christ,' in acceptance with the Father, makes you one with Him in His rejection by the world. The former you have by faith, the latter as a necessary consequence from the exhibited life of this faith.

Do you see yourself at the cross, forgiven all your trespasses? That blessed voice that acquitted you says, 'Go, and sin no more.' Do you see yourself at the cross, 'justified from all things,' and set down in perfect righteousness before God? Know, dear brother, that you have to justify your own profession of faith before men, by the good works of faith which they can understand and appreciate; and also you have to justify, before men, that God who you say has acquitted you and set you down before Himself, in His own righteousness, which is Christ.

Do you see yourself as one set apart by that blood which has been taken from the altar into ' the holiest of all,' and reckoned by God as one whose ' life is hid with Christ in God'? Know, dear brother, that you are to be purifying yourself, even as He is pure. Having His place of life and righteousness inside the veil, we feel it a high privilege to take His place of testimony and rejection outside the camp. In the language of faith, and regarding myself as God reckons me — once crucified, but now alive in Christ Jesus, I can say,—

> ' So nigh, so very nigh to God,
> I cannot nearer be;
> For in the person of His Son
> I am as near as He.'

And the necessary consequence of knowing this, and living in the power of it, will be a closer, holier walk with God; and my prayer and cry, the longing of my flesh-clogged soul, as I pant after conscious nearness, will ever be —

'Nearer, still nearer, Lord, my God,
I long to walk with Thee;
To know more fully Him I know,
My prayer, my joy shall be;
To live more like a ransomed child,
Till Christ Himself I see.'

Shall we not then, knowing that our ' citizenship is in heaven' (Phil. iii. 20), with the risen Christ as our rule, and his walk here as our example, soar upward, onward, and homeward — living above the world, the devil, and the flesh — 'strong in the grace that is in Christ Jesus,' having the 'joy of the Lord as our strength?'

Striving one, — Are you trying to perfect in the flesh that which has been begun in the Spirit? Do you count it a small matter that Christ has died for you, and that you are now in Him? What more can you have? You are conscientiously striving after holiness; but still you are constantly thinking and talking much more about the old man in you, than Christ for you and in you. Why is this? You are not reckoning as God has reckoned, and hence this useless warfare. There is a fight — the fight of faith, the fight I have as a saint against God's foes and mine, the world, the devil, and the flesh. This is ' a good fight.' There is also a most ignoble and Christ-dishonouring fight, a fight by which I try to make the flesh better; to purify the filthy fountain; to wash the rags of the prodigal instead of accepting the best robe— a living perfect, entire Christ. ' The just shall **live** by faith,' as well as be begotten by faith. Remember that there can be no holy walk with God unless I know that He has made me a son.

God is well pleased with Christ, why are you not pleased with Him?

'Ah!' you say, ' I am satisfied with Christ; but not with myself.'

Will you ever be pleased with yourself? Would it be well for you if you were so? Well, then, at once, by faith, adopt Paul's language, 'No longer I, but Christ' — Christ for me! Whether it were Paul or Peter, he had just to fall into the poor Gentile sinner's place, and plead, 'I am a sinner; therefore, Christ for me.' ' But I am not a great sinner,' you say.

He died for all kinds of sinners.

'But I am too great a sinner,' do you say?

Do you deserve to be nailed to a cross as an accursed thing? How far did Jesus descend to reach your case? Are there any steps needed to lead from your position to His? He was made a curse for us; He lay in the tomb, and you — ' dead in trespasses and sins ' — are lying in the tomb. Has he not come down to the very spot where you are? Are there any stepping stones needed between two, when both are lying side by side in the place of death? Ah, no; the gospel of Christ is — The Saviour for the sinner! Christ for me! God's way of life for my way of death!

He came down even to the grave, and became the dead One for me. I believe in Him, and, as one with Him, I leap at one bound straight out of my grave up to His throne. 'I am crucified with Christ, nevertheless I live; yet not I, but Christ liveth in me.' This is not a matter of feeling, but all a matter of faith, merely apprehending the grace of God, ' I live by the faith of the Son of God, who loved me and gave himself for me (Gal. ii. 20).

The moment you lose faith in your creed— 'for myself,' and have faith in God's — 'Christ for me.' you are 'born again' you are 'crucified with Christ,' and are now living in His risen life.

'Have no confidence in the flesh,' and then you will rejoice in Christ Jesus, and worship God in the Spirit,

With Christ we *died* to sin,	Rom. vi. 8.
Lay *buried* in His tomb;	Rom. vi. 4.
But *quicken'd* now with Him, our Life,	Eph. ii. 5.
We stand beyond our doom!	Rom. vi. 7.
Our God in wondrous love,	Eph. ii. 4..
Hath *raised* us, who were dead;	Eph. ii. 6.
And in the heavenlies, *made us sit*	Eph. ii. 6.
In Christ our living Head.	Eph. i. 22.
For us He now appears	Heb. ix. 24.
Within the veil above;	Heb. vi. 19.
Accepted, and complete in Him,	Eph. i. 6.
We triumph in His love.	Rom. viii. 39.
In Christ we now are made	1 Co. i. 30.
The righteousness of God;	2 Co. v. 21.
As sons of God, and *heirs* with Christ,	1 Jo. v. i.
We follow where He trod.	Col. iii. i.
Rejected and despised.	Is. liii. 3.
He bore the open shame;	Heb. xii. 2.
As *fellow-sufferers* journeying home,	Rom. viii, 17.
We glory in His name.	Acts v. 41.
Soon will the Bridegroom come,	Rev. xxii. 20.
His Bride from earth to call!	i Thes. iv. 16.
We, *glorified* with Him, shall reign,	Rev. . xx. 4.
Till God be all in all.	I Co. xv. 28.

The Devil

Our Adversary

DO not believe in eternal punishment, said a man one day to a friend of mine 'But that does not alter the fact,' replied my friend. This remark led to the man's conversion. Is it wise to shut the eye to danger.? We know best how to deal with a foe when we know all about himself, his plans, his tactics.

Wellington became the greatest conqueror b} knowing his enemies, their strength, and their stratagems. He is the skilled surgeon who has thought over all the possible dangers that may arise, and is prepared to meet them. When the builder of the Menai Bridge was suggesting various cautions, his coadjutors sometimes said to him that he was raising difficulties. 'No,' he answered, 'I'm solving them.' And so for every accident he was prepared.

In our spiritual conflict it is folly to despise the strength of our foes, it is wisdom to reckon on a power infinitely stronger. Many in the present day do not believe that there is a devil. They do not feel or realise any workings on their consciousness as of an external power. They think, therefore, that the devil is merely a word of the theologian, an expression that may be used to deceive and frighten children, but that intelligent men in this nineteenth century are not to be so deceived. With their friends of old they ' say that there is neither angel nor spirit' (Acts xxiii. 8). But this does not alter the fact that there is a devil. Men may conscientiously, and therefore strongly, believe a lie. In fact we find, in 2 Thess. ii. 10, that because men 'received not the love of tiie truth that they might be saved, for this cause God shall send them strong delusions that they should believe a lie, that they all might be damned who believed not the truth but had pleasure in unrighteousness.'

Others who believe, from the teaching of Scripture, that there is a devil, have little knowledge of his personality. They do not seem to realise that he is as truly a person, though invisible, as the Son of God, his great opponent. They think of Satan as a mere influence or powder. They tell us that they have devil enough when they have their own evil heart. And true enough, it is 'deceitful above all things, and incurably wicked.' But that Satan is a present, scheming, watchful, cunning being, going about seeking our destruction, is realised by few; and by those few very imperfectly.

REV. XII.

In the twelfth chapter of Revelation we have depicted a remarkable series of his workings. May the Lord open up to our minds from this passage the reality of his existence as a person, the subtlety and determination of his plans, and the power that has been provided to meet him at every step.

I do not now enter into the interpretation of this graphic scene, however blessed it may be to the soul that reads and understands it; but I would rather try to glean a few practical lessons from the moral truths revealed to us in this picture, which, in all its details, has yet to be fulfilled. Before adducing these, I would merely glance at the characters that figure in the scene, that in gathering these lessons we may not confuse the mind of the intelligent reader who is looking for a deeper and closer rendering of it.

In chap. xi. 19, the temple of God is open in heaven (for Jesus and His elders are now seen as there since chap.iv.), and *the ark* of His covenant is shown as token of His grace, and the *lightning,* as token of His judgment, before we are introduced to the great scene of chap. xii. We are told who the dragon is, verse 9, ' That old serpent, called the devil and Satan, who deceiveth the whole world ' — like the *aliases* of a habit-and-repute criminal. The man-child, from Ps. ii.,Isa. ix. 6, &c., is evidently Jesus, ver. 5, 'a man-child who was to rule all nations with a rod of iron.' His mother, in symbolic language, of course, being Israel, from whom, according to the flesh, Christ was born, seen as the faithful remnant persecuted and preserved through the tribulation of the short 1260 days after Satan has been cast out of heaven — where the saints have been seen seated (chap iv.) — to the earth, where he is in great wrath, for his time is short ere he be chained in the pit.

I. The Devourer.

Read the 4th verse of this twelfth chapter: 'And the Dragon stood before the woman which was ready to be delivered, for to devour her child as soon as it was born.'

Jesus is said to be born King of the Jews in Matt. i. Look at chap, ii.: there we find the devil's first attempt to devour Him as soon as He was born. Herod, his tool, slew 'all the children that were in Bethlehem and in all the coasts thereof from two years old and under,' and the weeping of Rachel is the sad witness to the devil's awful power, but through the almighty wisdom of God the young child's life is spared. Thwarted in this murderous plan, he comes with plausible temptation, trying to make Him leave the place of the Sent One and the Servant; but the Word of God made him flee for a season. In Gethsemane we again find Satan; but last and most awful of all, we see this great dragon, the serpent, at Calvary, bruising His heel, trying to hold Him in his death-hold, wounding Him with his venomed sting. The devourer feels now sure of his prey. Jesus is in the jaws of death. Chains of hell are around him. ' Shall the prey be taken from the mighty, shall the lawful captive be delivered. 'Yes: there is a greater power than the mighty one here, there is the Almighty. There is a power higher than even that seen in Creation or Providence; there is the power of coming out from under death — laying down the life and taking it up again. 'Through death He destroyed him that had the power of death, that is the devil.' Not only has Satan failed to devour the Prince of Life, but he has got his head bruised. This is the venomous serpent on the pole, whose power has thus been destroyed by the Son of man lifted up (John iii.) The sting has been wrenched from the serpent's jaws. The keys of death and the grave are now hung at the girdle of the glorious Conqueror, who has fought the fight alone, by weakness showing Himself to be Almighty.

'By weakness and defeat
  He won the mead and crown;
Trod all our foes beneath His feet,
  By being trodden down.

'He hell in hell laid low;
  Made sin, He sin o'erthrew;
Bow'd to the grave, destroy'd it so,
  And death by dying slew.'

'For this purpose the Son of God was manifested, that He might destroy the works of the devil.' (i John iii. 8.) The Lord is risen, yea. He is ascended as a man, a glorified man, beyond the power of Satan. He is seated as the subject One. The servant who undertook for man has been 'caught up unto God and to His throne,' and we find that this is the deliverance that is mentioned in Rev. xii. 5. It is a question now to be settled between Satan and the God who has raised Jesus up, between the power of Satan and the throne-power of the Almighty God. Justice and power have vindicated Christ's title to bruise the serpent's head, and take His position as man, the highest in heaven on God's own throne.

The serpent in Eden tempted the woman and ruined mankind. God said, ' I will put enmity between thee and the woman, between thy seed and her seed.' Blessed be God, He has put the enmity, and it cannot be taken away. What a fearful friendship it would have been if God had left man in the friendship that Adam began with Satan! All along the stream of time Satan has been at his devouring work. To-day he is 'going about as a roaring lion, seeking whom he may *devour*.' Do we realise this? It surely means something. I believe it means far more than we suppose. By how many different ways does he accomplish this! If he can keep people in their natural state of death, he is as sure of his prey as if he had them with him in everlasting burning. If he can lull them, soothe them, deceive them, blind them, he has them sure, and they will be an easy prey.

He knows that life is communicated by the Spirit applying the *word* of the living God,— that word that tells of a victorious Conqueror, a risen Christ, of Him who liveth and was dead, and is alive again for evermore. That word links the believer to Him who was caught up to God's throne, and tells him that he is identified with the victorious conqueror of death, that he is united to death's master. Wherefore, Satan is very busy when the gospel of God is preached, so we read that there is a class of people that hear the word: 'then cometh the devil, and taketh away *the word* out of their hearts, *lest* they should believe and be saved.' (Luke viii. 12.) What a devil-like intention! Does every preacher of the gospel realise this, that such an enemy is among his audience? Does every hearer realise it, that such a seemingly simple thing may leave him in the jaws of Satan for ever. If men do not believe that they must be born again, in order to enter the Kingdom of God, Satan does. If men do not believe that the ' entrance of the word gives light,' Satan does. He takes this word away lest it save them. Satan is a clever theologian. He knows the Bible: he believes it, he can quote it, he can use it for his own fiendish ends. After the gospel is preached, he is ever ready to snatch away the word. ' What did you think of that preacher?' is the common introduction, after the gospel is preached, to a series of criticisms on his merits and demerits, and a pretty sure token that in the discussion concerning the messenger the message is to be forgotten. '*Lest* they should believe and be saved!' If Satan can keep out that seed, he will let the man cultivate the field, be very attentive to it, water it, spend much time on it: in plain words, he will let men be moral and philanthropic, be religious, and make profession, contend stoutly for sound orthodoxy, and clever theology, if he can keep out the seed of life.

Satan knows that there is life in a look at the crucified One, therefore he will let the wounded sinner apply ointments and plasters, and all sorts of palliatives to his sin-bitten soul; but will use all his power to keep him from beholding the Lamb of God. A look at the brazen serpent cured those bitten by fiery serpents — a look at Him who destroyed the great serpent's power, immediately and for ever saves those who are ready to be devoured by the mighty dragon, for ' as Moses lifted up the serpent in the wilderness, even so must the Son of man be lifted up, that whosoever believeth in Him should not perish, but have eternal life.' By many devices the great deceiver succeeds in hiding this life-giving cross; for ' If our gospel be hid, it is hid to them that are lost: in whom the *god of this world* hath blinded the minds of them which believe not, *lest* the light of the glorious gospel of Christ who is the image of God, should shine unto them.' Truly, O Apollyon, Abaddon, thou art the deceiver of the whole world. What fools men are! Reader, are you led captive at his will; are you in his meshes, within the teeth of his jaws, ready to be devoured? Are you not only led captive of your lusts, but bound hand and foot by Satan?

Believing reader, in Jesus thou art safe. He is at God's throne; thou art there in Him; this is thy safety. God's throne is safe, he cannot devour it, therefore he cannot devour thee. He has done his utmost as to devouring thee; he is eternally foiled. His power is broken. The poison, the cruelty of the great dragon, that old serpent, have been met and overcome by the 'Lamb in the midst of the throne.'

Is 'the evil one,' 'the wicked one' thy destroyer?— 'The Holy One' is thy preserver.

Is 'the angel of the bottomless pit' at thy back with his belching flame? — 'The King of Glory' is the Captain of thy salvation.

Is the knife of him that is 'a murderer from the beginning' whetted to be plunged into thy bosom? — ' The Prince of Life' is thy life.

Is ' the prince of darkness ' trying to enwrap thy soul?—'The Light of Life' surrounds thy goings.

Does Satan come as an angel of light? — We have received the blessed Spirit, by whom we can detect his wiles; we are not ignorant of his devices. Let us be sober and vigilant against such a foe. We have to pick our steps. Being now in Christ, soon we shall be ' caught up ' in reality, body and soul, entirely and for ever beyond his power, wiles, devices, and snares. Yes, we shall be caught up together with all the saints of Jesus, to meet our Conqueror in the air, and be ever with Him; and 'the God of peace shall bruise Satan under your feet shortly.' (Rom. xvi. 20.)

After he is thus foiled, and cannot *devour* us, does he leave us? Nay! But we find Satan in this same twelfth chapter (ver. 10), as

II. The Accuser.

'He **ACCUSES** the brethren before God day and night.' Michael and his angels are to cast him down to the earth at the beginning of the times of great trial, but meantime he is there, not certainly in the ' light,' God's dwelling-place, in the third, the highest, heaven, but as the Prince of the Power of the Air, having power to stand before God and accuse the brethren. That Satan has access into God's presence may startle some who have not thought about it; but it is the teaching of Scripture, i Kings xxii. 21, shews that a lying spirit appeared before God, to put lies into the mouths of Ahab's advisers.

Again, in Job i. 6, we read — 'Now there was a day when the sons of God came to present themselves before the Lord, and Satan came also among them,' to accuse Job. In Zech. iii. it is written — ' He shewed me Joshua the high priest standing before the angel of the Lord, and Satan standing at his right hand to resist him.' In Eph. vi. 12 — 'We wrestle not against flesh and blood, but against...spiritual wickedness in *heavenly* places.' Day and night, dear fellow-Christians, he has access to God, and accuses us before Him; sometimes truly, alas! How often does he first tempt and then accuse! How much failure of ours can he put his hand upon! and besides he is a slanderer, a false accuser. He is not the accuser of the world, but only of ' the brethren,' but he ' deceiveth the whole world.'

What is our strength? 'If any man sin, we have an advocate with the Father,' one who never slumbers nor sleeps. We speak much, and we cannot dwell too much, upon the finished work of Jesus; but how precious is the unfinished, untiring, unremittent work of our blessed Lord! If the accuser speaks of sin, He points to the blood, that with which, for us, He has entered into the heavens.

'He is Jesus Christ the righteous, and He is the propitiation for our sins.' The accuser has to find fault with Him, for we are in Him. Nothing short of this appeal to the presented blood will silence his insinuations and overcome his accusations. So it is said (ver. 11), 'They overcame him by the *blood* of the Lamb.' Saints do not cast him out of heaven; angels do that, but the brethren overcome him while he is there, and is accusing them. This is before God.

In my own experience of all his accusations I bring the sword of the Spirit, the Word of God, apart from all my feelings and states, and say to all his accusings, as to his temptations, ' It is written.' Thus Jesus overcame him when he was on earth, therefore it is said that not only ' they overcame him by the blood of the Lamb,' but also by 'the *word* of their testimony.' 'Resist the devil and he will flee from you' — for he is a coward at heart; ' neither give place to the devil.' The blood and the word shut his mouth for ever, and are the answer to his gravest accusations, be they true or false. Though our sins are as scarlet, Jesus points to the blood, and they become 'white as snow;' 'red like crimson,' He says they become as wool. 'If we confess our sins. He is faithful' — why? because His word has said it — 'and just' — why? because of the *blood* presented — ' to forgive us our sins, and to cleanse us from all unrighteousness.' The blood of Jesus Christ *cleanseth* us from **all** sin.

Is the father of lies against us? — the living Truth is for us. Is he desiring to sift us as wheat?—Jesus is constantly praying that our faith may never fail us, for by that shield we can quench all Satan's fiery darts, meet all his accusations, and, in the calm consciousness of eternal peace with God, wait upon Him, do His commandments, and receive the power that will make us love not our lives unto death. (Rev. xii. ii.)

He cannot *devour* us: we are in Christ.

He is overcome when He *accuses* us; Christ's blood is for us. Does he leave us? No. He exercises his power against us now, as

III. The Persecutor.

Read Rev. xii. 13. 'When the dragon saw that he was cast unto the earth he *persecuted* the woman.' And here his cunning is taxed to its utmost; varying with times and peoples, tastes and civilisation. His manner changes, but the rank venom of his sting is always the same — the deluge from his mouth always poured upon us. lie brings into his service all kinds of tools; the stake, the inquisition, the scaffold in one age; more refined but as real persecution in another; the ill-will and planning of the world, and what is worse than all. the evil-speaking and slandering of fellow-Christians. Individually, beloved friends, let us ask, are we washing one another's feet, or advancing Satan's work, being used as his tools in speaking evil of those things that Ave know not? You may know what it is to be misunderstood, misrepresented, maligned, looked at with suspicion by a fellow-Christian, and may have felt it to be the direst persecution, more painful than thumbscrews; — watch and pray lest

107

you in turn be thus used against others. We do not feel the reality of the common adversary, else we should be all more united and of one accord, continuing in brotherly love. Soldiers may have their disputes, quarrels, and even duels, when in the barracks and on home service, but on the battle-field the bitterest are shoulder to shoulder against one common foe.

Against all his persecutions, what is the provision? ver. 14, power for flight to the wilderness, and being fed there by God. He has given us of His Spirit. The spirit of truth and sonship. He has shut us into the wilderness, and there we have found Himself our provision. A quaint old divine used to say, ' the devil acts like a bull-dog to bark at us, and drive us closer to Christ.' The Psalms are the experience of David in the place of the poor man in the wilderness finding his all in God. What a blessed thing that Satan's persecutions but drive us nearer to our only good! The wilderness is the happiest place, when we get there, from the hand of our living, loving Father, His own manna, His own drink, and the guidance of His pillar cloud. Christ is all.

'In the desert, God will teach thee
   What the God that thou hast found,
Patient, gracious, powerful, holy,
   All His grace shall there abound.

'Though thy way be long and dreary,
   Eagle strength He'll still renew;
Garments fresh, and feet unweary,
   Tell how God hath brought thee
through.'

To be alone with God — to be in the wilderness with God — to be fed by God. Is this not life? is this not joy? It was better to be with David on the lonely hill-side, than with Saul in his costly palaces. Manna, water, and guidance are all I need; what more could I take, for this is Jesus, God's own joy, God's own delight, God's own rest, day by day, new every day, it cannot be kept for to-morrow; yesterday's will not do for to-day. How the hatred of the devil brings glory to God!

His *devourings* bring us to the 'caught up' Christ, and are thus met by *life in victory.*

His *accusations* bring us to the ' blood of the Lamb,' and are met by *life taken for us.*

His *persecutions* bring us to the wilderness provisions, and are met by *life nourished.*

After all this we have nothing more to fear, we can fear no evil, God is with us, as above and independent of all circumstance we find God for us, a table spread in the wilderness in presence of our enemies. He may still show his venom after he is thoroughly defeated, for we next find him as

IV. The Blasphemer.

This seen in Rev. xiii. 5, 6, in the person of the beast to whom Satan gives power. 'He opened his mouth in blasphemy against God to blaspheme His name and His tabernacle, and them that dwell in heaven.' But blasphemies can do us little harm. We need no fortification against them. At school we have seen the big boy that used to lord it over all the little ones subdued, conquered, and on the ground. In his defeat he could only call bad names, which he knew could do no harm. Even though Satan slay the body, this touches not our life — it is hid with Christ in God. Can he devour

108

that? It is because of the name we bear that the blasphemies of hell are poured upon us. There are the 'synagogues of Satan,' in which the blasphemous doctrines of devils are taught. We fear not the servants of Satan, though homage on all sides be paid to him by all classes, in their business and pleasure, and the crowns of earth be laid at his feet.

Those whose names are written from the foundation of the world in the book of the Lamb slain, can listen to his blasphemies, can rejoice in the Lord, though he should slay their bodies, and they can afford to wait for their inheritance.

What can I now say, unsaved sinner, to you? You are in the *jaws of the devil*. He is your father: is he to be your tormentor day and night for ever in that awful hell which was never prepared for you, but 'prepared for the devil and his angels?' Look at the judgment of the living nations, the contrast between the blessing and cursing — 'blessed of my Father,' but not cursed of my Father — 'Kingdom prepared for you,' but fire prepared for the devil and his angels.' One, look outward to Jesus and you are saved; not a look inward to a feeling that can give nothing but despair to the conscientious soul. God has given you Jesus, and in Him is all. Are you not satisfied with Jesus for you? God is.

Fellow believer, rejoice in the Lord: the greatest enemy's power is broken: soon he will really and as to fact, as he is already judicially and to faith, be bruised beneath thy feet. Jesus is thine, and all His power and dominion, and might, and glory, and inheritance, arc thine, and, above all, His heart, His love, Himself, is thine.

In Him we conquer the devourer;
In Him we overcome the accuser;
In Him we defy the persecutor;
In Him we are beyond the blasphemer. 'More than conquerors through Him that loved us.'

Come with your weakness and find shelter in the all-powerful Jesus.

Eph. vi. 11-18.

Be strong in Jehovah, though hard be the fight,
We'll conquer, we know, in the power of His might;
Put on the whole armour of God every one,
For it alone shelters till victory's won.

Thus we sing while we march through the midst of our foes,
Who stand all determined our way to oppose;
We shall conquer their legion, our battle song raise;
The Lord is our Captain; his name ever praise.

Thus armed we shall stand and shall meet Satan's wiles;
We know his devices, the world he beguiles;
It is not against flesh and blood that we fight,
But powers that would force us from heavenly light

With loins girt with truth may we stand in the fight,
And righteousness placed as our breastplate so bright;
Our feet shod with sandals prepared for the war,
The gospel of peace which our foes shall not mar.

Above all Faith's shield we must grasp 'gainst our foe.
By it we shall quench every dart Satan throws;
Salvation our helmet, bestowed by our Lord,
The sword of the Spirit His conquering word.

"The trumpet is sounding, the trumpet of war,
Not peace while we wait for our bright morning Star;
We watch where the foe would surprise or alarm,
By prayer we shall nerve for the fight every arm.

Lord, give us more faith thus to meet every foe,
Thus Satan is conquered and shall be laid low;
This, this is the triumph o'er earth and its gain
O'er sin still within, but which never shall reign.

Serving the Lord!

Our Work.

I WAS very much interested lately, in reading the life of Dr. Chalmers, to see how many years he preached the gospel to others, and, by his own confession, was still unconverted. I thought of that text, 'lest *preaching* to others I myself should be a castaway.' Paul does not say, ' lest after being *born again*. I should be a castaway; ' we know that this is impossible. But a man may preach with the most powerful eloquence to others, and still be unsaved. Many in this Christian land begin very early to engage in some good work. At a certain time they become members of the church, as it is said; alas! how often not knowing whether they are saved or not. They then may take a young class in the *Sabbath* school, have a district to visit, look after the affairs of the church, or the necessities of the poor, become, perhaps a deacon and then an elder, or it may be a preacher, and all this time they may have never had this matter definitely, finally, conclusively settled, 'Am I saved?' They trust they are on the right road to be saved, which of course is the leading idea in all legalism, ritualism and popery, and an entire ignoring of the Bible method.

Some do the best they can, and strive, it may be, with prayers and tears and resolutions and determinations, *in order* to get into God's favour, and thereby in the long run to receive eternal life, with the pardon of all their sins.

Others work and do the best they can, and strive as the former, *because* they know they are accepted already — *because* they know they have the pardon of all their sins — *because* they know they *have* eternal life. The former is false service, the latter is true.

I. False Service.

There are those who believe in justification by faith, and other doctrines of grace, and who yet think that if they do their duty, and try to serve God as sincerely and faithfully as they can. He will, at the last, overlook their many failures, in some vague

110

way or other, for Christ's sake, and reward them for the good deeds which they have done, and give them at the judgment day everlasting life.

Now, this is quite a mistake, and arises from a total misapprehension of God's character and man's condition. God's character is perfect, and before I can be engaged in acceptable service I must be in harmony with this character. In order to be a proper servant of God, I must *start with being perfectly accepted* by God.

Man's position is not that of one who is only a little out of God's mind, and who by a few sincere and vigorous efforts maybe put right; but of one who is really dead, so far as connection with God is concerned. He is separated from God, and therefore from truth, from goodness, from life. In God is all truth, all goodness, all life; outside of Him there is none: Man, by nature, is born out of fellowship with God, and therefore he has no.t the slightest power to serve God acceptably, for he has not the- life that can move in the direction of God, and in which he can serve Him. The movements in Christian service of an unconverted man are the galvanic movements of a corpse, which may seem very energetic; yet, alas, it is but a corpse that moves! All Scripture and experience tell us these two truths concerning God's character and man's condition.

Wherefore, dear friend, unless thou hast been born again, quickened into a new life from death, thou canst not serve God acceptably. Thou mayest strive day and night in all sincerity, but thou art dead; thou mayest visit the sick and minister to the dying (the holiest privileges of the saved one); all is vain; thou mayest comfort and assist the widow and the fatherless, and have the prayers of many an orphan for thy reward, and yet be no better as to thy standing before God than the profligate and the profane; thou mayest give of thy bread to the poor; thou mayest support the cause of Christ in all its missions and churches at home and abroad-; thou mayest give half of thy income to the advancement of the Lord's work, and not one penny stand to thy credit before God. Cain's sacrifice, beautiful, fair, and lovely as it was, and presented by a man who was at that time a professor of religion, and a sincere worshipper, was rejected by God. And so it is still. God will reject you and your sacrifice unless you come as one at peace with Him through His sacrifice and not as one coming to make friends with God by your sacrifice. If you are out of Christ, your good deeds as well as your bad deeds are an abomination to God. All your 'righteousnesses are as *filthy* rags' (Isa. Ixiv. 6), not only failing to cover you, but *defiling* you. '*Whatsoever* is not of faith is sin' (Rom. xiv. 23). You may be true to your friends; you may do your duty as parents, and provide for your own; but it is all sin: for, as saith the Scripture, ' the ploughing of the wicked is sin' (Prov. xxi. 4). Every action, however commendable in the Christian, and however much binding upon you as a moral duty, is reckoned by God, if done by you, to be a sin, because it is the action of one not at peace with Him through His own peace. ' Without faith it is impossible to please God (Heb. xi. 6). This is God's theology, however hard it may seem, and however much opposed to your ideas, and to the prevailing ideas of the world concerning good works and their reward. 'Dead works' is stamped on all your deeds. Until you serve God as one who is saved, all your service will but intensify your anguish in the pit of woe, whither the Christless, the seemingly good and fair, beautiful and noble, are all swept together with the vile, the loathsome, the idolater, the profane. There are not two hells. Where will you spend eternity.?

II. True Service.

Half an hour ago you may have been serving in the dark, as an unforgiven one, and, during the next half hour, you may pass from death unto life, and thus stand on the ground of the accepted servant. God is perfect: to meet God I must meet Him in perfection. There is no perfection in me; but He has provided the means by which each of us may at once become acceptable *servants*, by first becoming accepted *sons*. Jesus, His only-begotten and well-beloved Son, eternally in the Father's bosom, took upon Him our nature, descended to our place of responsibility and service, and approved Himself to be the perfect Servant in that very place m which we had failed; became sin for us, was obedient unto death, having gone through all the billows of God's wrath, has been raised from the dead, and is now at the Father's right hand. If, therefore, we become by faith identified with Him, we can see in Him all our responsibilities under law met; we can look into His empty grave, and reckon our sins buried there; and now, as those who are beyond the doom of sin, and beyond its judgment, we can serve in ' newness of life,' a resurrection-life. This, and nothing else, is the foundation of true service, the service of love, the service of sons: for we now stand in Christ's place of sonship as He once, in grace, occupied our place of death.

We ask you, is this not a real vantage ground for service? What a wretched, menial service it is to be working hard for life, and doubting whether it can ever be obtained! The true service is a working *from* the Cross, not *to* the Cross. The corpse does not bestir itself to get life, but it is the living man who works because he has life. Be not deceived. This is God's plan; *life*, then *service*. Ask yourselves now the question, 'Am I serving because I have life? because I am saved?' Then it is evident that you know you are saved — you '*know* that you are of God.' (i John V. 19.)

But perhaps some one maybe thinking, 'Well, I've been doing this little and that little, but I have never been conscious of being born again.' Stop, then, dear friend, at once, and make it sure. Turn on the spot from thy service, and get rid of thy sin by believing in Him who, as the perfect servant, bare our sins in His own body on the tree. (i Peter ii. 24.) Get into Christ — in His perfection thou canst meet and serve the living God.

'But,' you may ask, 'how am I to get into Him?' Simply by knowing Him (John xvii. 3); by believing on Him (John iii. 36); by trusting in Him (2 Tim. i. 12). God has given Him to you already. (John iii. 16.) You do not require to go to heaven to beseech God to send you Jesus to die for sin. (Rom. x. 6.) No! 'For God so loved the world that He gave His only-begotten Son.' And Christ dieth no more. In the love-gift of God, Jesus is yours. If you go to hell, it must be over *a given* Christ.

When the poor men in the cotton manufacturing districts were starving, moved with pity you sent your money to the committee for distributing bread to them. Now, suppose some poor man, with his wife and children sitting in their empty room, the last of their furniture having been sold for bread — a few stones for seats, and a bunch of straw their bed; no fire on the hearth; no crust of bread in the cupboard, the last having been consumed a couple of days before; children crying for bread; the mother's eyes refusing to weep; the father's skeleton hands clasped in anguish; no bread, and no work; starvation, dire starvation staring them in the face I A knock is heard at the door, a man comes in with a loaf and lays it on the table, and says, '*That is yours*, for the people of Britain have so pitied you that they have sent this bread. Rise, eat, rejoice, and starve no more.' Suppose that poor man would neither touch the loaf himself, nor let his wife nor children taste it, but said, ' How can it be mine? I never got a pennyworth of bread but by the sweat of my brow; there must be some mistake. I cannot take this; not having wrought for it, it cannot be mine.' Everybody would have shouted, '*Eat, man! eat,* and ask no questions, for you are starving, and the messenger's word is enough. He said the loaf was yours.'

Fellow-sinner, this is but a faint picture of *your condition* and *God's provision.* **JE-SUS,** His perfect provision for the soul's need, has been sent, has suffered for sin, and has gone back in righteousness to the Father. Are you not on the edge of eternal damnation, and do you begin to ask questions about your warrant to take Christ? He is yours in the gift of God. Yea. more, God *commands* you to use Him (i John iii. 23). Dare you-disobey God by continuing unsaved?

How can I serve the Lord until I can say, ' He is *my* Lord?'

A gentleman had paid his money for the ransom of a slave, and had given her her freedom. She had been born a slave, and knew not what freedom meant. Her tears fell fast on the signed parchment which her deliverer brought to prove it to her; she only looked at him with fear. At last he got ready to go his way, and as he told her what she must do when he was gone, it did dawn on her what freedom was. With the first breath, 'I will follow him,' she said: ' I will follow him; I will serve him all my days;' and to every reason against it she only cried, ' He redeemed me I He redeemed me! He redeemed me!'

When strangers used to visit that master's house, and noticed, as all did, the loving constant service of the glad-hearted girl, and asked her why she was so eager with unbidden service, night by night, and day by day, she had but one answer, and she loved to give it,—

'He redeemed me! He redeemed me! He redeemed me!'

Is this *your* motive-power for serving God — 'He redeemed me?'—or is it only, 'Well, I hope I may yet be found among the redeemed, and meanwhile I do the best I can?' Wretched slavery, with the chain of death or doubt hanging on the limbs! Rather take God at His word now, and joyfully exclaim, ' O Lord, truly I am Thy servant... Thou hast loosed my bonds' (Psalm cxvi. i6).

III. A Word to Fellow-Servants.

I would now speak a word to you who are fellow-workers for, and fellow-sufferers with, Jesus. It is only now that we can have fellowship with Him in His service as the rejected of earth. Let us then be instant in season, out of season.'

'He redeemed me!' Let it be written as with letters of gold on every page of our diary. While in your mission of love you visit the poor, the sick, and the dying, may it ever be your first work to point them to Jesus. While in every way striving to alleviate misery, even if it were by giving but a cup of cold water, let the main thing be to speak of Jesus. Be careful ever to have the single eye, and do nothing to be seen of men. Do nothing to men; do all to God; and have no master but your Redeemer. Be bound to serve by no chain but that of love. If a great sphere be denied you, occupy the small one. If it is not yours to preach to hundreds or thousands, be like Him who spent a sultry noon under a scorching sun by the well side, that He might impart the water of life to a worthless woman. ' Whatsoever thy hand findeth to do, do it with thy might;' do not wait for to-morrow and for some great opportunity, but do the little service, whatever it may be, do it *now*. Draw all your strength from God, depending on Him alone.

The great work is that which is done on individual responsibility — ' My own work.' Jesus says, ' Whatsoever ye shall ask the Father in my name, He will give you.' (John xvi. 23.) ' *Whatsoever,*' without limit, without restraint, without bound, so that you may ask anything you please. Dear fellow-worker, do you feel as if this were too much, and say, 'I cannot have God's arm so under my will?' It is, nevertheless, true. What! can a creature thus prevail with the Creator? Yes, indeed, and the reason is, that we have been made ' partakers of the divine nature ' (2 Pet. i. 4), because before God we are as Jesus is — as near, as dear. We are *in* Him, and being in Him, every request, proceeding from this new nature, is in perfect harmony with the Divine Mind.

We may well say with such a petition. What grace, Lord! what condescension! what love! Thou hast not spared Thy Son! Thou hast made me one with Him. Thou hast said, whatsoever I will I shall receive; and Therefore, Lord, my will is *whatsoever Thou wilt*. I give Thee back Thy behest. It is too much for me to bear, and now, from the very depths of my soul, I pray, 'Father, "Thy will be done!" Lead me in Thy will; may everything I do be in Thy mind;' and then, *asking* will but be the promptings of that divine life in me, and *receiving* but the natural issue from the hand of Him who is the fountain of that life. What a service of joy! Such a life has no outward bustle and noise, no running hither and thither, but, like the light, it cannot be hid. Quietly it beams wherever it exists. It is calm as the gentle heat of the summer sun noiselessly warming all around. Thus energised by the life from above, meet parent and child, friend and neighbour, rich and poor, and the brighter will be your ' crown of righteousness.' Servants faithful to their earthly masters shall receive the reward of the inheritance at the judgment-seat of Christ. (Col. iii. 24.) It will then appear that it was better to have spoken 'five words' (i Cor. xiv. 19) for God, than to have spoken 'ten thousand words' to make 'a fair shew in the flesh' (Gal. vi. 12), and please men; better to have been eloquent for God in the calm silence of a life pointing to Jesus, than to have made earth ring with high-sounding words and world-patching schemes.

'It was not any word that was ever spoken to me,' said an old and oft-approved servant of God to a brother in the Lord, from whom I heard the narrative; ' it was no word that wakened me up from my death of sin, but the moving of a dying man's finger. My mother had often prayed for me, and tried to lead me to Jesus; but I hated God, and when I escaped from her control grew to be a wild sinner and such a bold infidel that all her godly friends were afraid to see me; but, in the providence of God, I was left to watch alone by the bedside of a tailor, a poor deformed fellow, when he lay a-dying. He had often spoken to me of Jesus, but I had never heeded him more than my mother, or any of the others. When I was nursing him there that day, he plead with me many times to mind my soul, but I was perfectly hard; all he could say had no effect. But at last, when the death-rattle was in his throat, and I saw he could speak no longer, he just raised his hand and pointed with his finger to the sky. *That* stirred me, and I had no rest till Jesus gave me rest.'

The judgment-seat is coming. Fellow-Christian, no question will be raised there about thy standing, about thy salvation. As to safety thou art already passed from death unto life, and wilt not come into judgment; but as to service, thy works will be judged. The judgment is by fire. Whatsoever stands that trial stands to thy credit—if nothing stands, then thy works will all be lost though thou thyself art saved as by fire.

There are two kinds of works — one class symbolized in scripture under the heading of wood, hay, stubble; the other gold, silver, precious stones. Every work is on one side or the other. You will observe that wood, hay, and stubble are greatest in quantity. But it is not quantity that the fire regards; a ton of hay is as easily and as surely burned as a pound. Many in our day have the greatest regard for quantity — great works, much activity. How little the striving after the pure gold, the silver, and the precious stones! How mixed is the life-work of the best man! A layer of wood, a grain of gold, then a large quantity of hay, then a little silver, plenty of stubble, how few precious stones: but the fire sifts all! At that awful catastrophe at Abergele, where railway carriages and living men and women were burned to ashes, diamonds, gold watches, and silver ornaments were found afterwards among the rubbish. The peer could not be distinguished from the servant; wood could not be separated from bone; but the diamond was still bright, and the gold and silver still precious. What a happy day is coming to every Christian! He will be so glad to see in one blaze, as upon one funeral pile, all that in his life ever dishonoured his Lord, or was not done with the single eye: only that will reappear in glory, which was to God's glory here, and he, already glorified, can at that tribunal appreciate nothing but what is in harmony with glory.

When at school our great ambition was to be first in the class. Who will be first then of all the class of Christians? Very different will be God's order then from our order now! The great of earth and preachers (even those who were of greatest eminence) perhaps giving place to some poor old starving widow, or some little child. I am convinced that many of those who are called great and well known and honoured Christians, will in that day, as to reward for the single eye, be far behind some poor, weak, despised ones of earth, whose power was in the secret place with God. God judges with righteous judgment.

Rich Christian, what of thy gold then? will it be accounted stubble in the glory? or art thou exchanging it now into the currency of heaven? Were I to travel in a foreign land, I could not get on very well with my British money. Even in England those coming from Scotland find it difficult to exchange Scotch notes. Before we go abroad we change as much money as we may require into the coin of that realm. Friend, this is for what thy life here is still given: ' Make to yourselves friends of the mammon of unrighteousness, that when ye fail they may receive you into everlasting habitations.' So said the Master, and many disciples have wondered and not understood the passage. It is simply ' Exchange your money into the currency of heaven.'

'The mammon of unrighteousness;' that is to say, in the Jewish economy it was a sign of a righteous man that his basket and store were full, that he had plenty of cattle, that he was rich. Now since Christ's rejection it is not so. The unrighteous have

God's money in this age. The normal lot of the Christian is poverty; nowhere to lay the head, since there was 'no room in the inn' for the Master. But suppose a man with a large fortune gets converted; what is he to do with this mammon of unrighteousness? Is he to hoard it up and add to it, and die a rich man? Nay. Is he at once and heedlessly to throw it away? Nay. He is to make it his friend. Exchange it into the coin of heaven. If he waits till he dies, none can be put into his coffin that will arise with him. But there is a method of sending it on before: the Lord has taught it. How many cups of cold water can it buy? These count, if given with the single eye. How many Bibles and missionaries to the heathen? Ten thousand channels are easily found when wanted. Whatever you do, make your money not your enemy, as it will be if you use it for self, but your friend, so that when you are done with money it may not be done with you, but will be standing to meet you in a new dress, in the gold and silver and precious stones at the throne, in the 'Well done' of the Master. Poor brother, thy poverty is no bar. One talent well used is more than ten abused, and money is but a poor talent.

It is not an occasional or periodic earnestness that God desires, but a calm, constant life-long work. A man moving about this world with the Holy Ghost within him, prepared for anything, at every step, by every look and word, testifying for his Lord, conscious of no effort, but living in calm peace with his Saviour God, in the unhindered power of an inner life, in the patient hope of a glory soon to dawn, is the type of God's true servant. His service does not depend on his rank, his circumstances, his position: these are all subservient to what the man is. He may be the wealthiest in the world, or have to sweep a street, but his joy in the service is the same. Such will have a natural entrance into the courts above, where the servants serve their Lord day and night.

O send me forth, my Saviour,
O send me for Thy glory,
Regarding not the praise of man,
And trampling on the fear of man,
And fighting for Thy glory, Thy glory.

There is a man who often stands
Between me and Thy glory,
His name is self,
My carnal self,

Self-seeking self,
Stands 'twixt me and Thy glory.

O mortify him, mortify him.
Put him down, my Saviour,
Exalt thyself alone: lift high
The banner of the cross,
And in its folds
Conceal the standard-bearer.

Dear fellow-servant, get so accustomed to serve your Lord Jesus Christ and Him alone, that your entrance into glory will not be unnatural, and thus an abundant entrance will be yours.

Every child of God, great and small, has a work; his or her own work. A brother in the Lord greatly surprised an old bed-ridden follower of the Lord by coming in with a smile to her one day, and saying,—

'I've got some work for you to do.'

'Me! what work! what can I do?'

'Oh, there's a little district meeting to be started, and you are to have special charge of it in praying about it.'

She got deeply interested in the people attending the little meeting, and this work did her and them much good. I saw a young boy confined to bed one day, and I told him he had a work to do. He had found Jesus, but he looked a little surprised. ' You have to pray and preach,' I said.— He smiled in surprise. — 'Yes, you have to pray for those that carry forth the gospel, and you have to lie there and preach sermons to all that come in, sermons on faith, patience, meekness, gentleness, adorning on your back, as we on our feet ought to do, the doctrine of God our Saviour.' The same thought came also from the lips of another young disciple, now in the presence of the Lord, waiting the resurrection beauty in which he will be clothed with all those who have been faithful unto death — who have endured to the end. He said, 'We *all* must speak for Jesus,' when it was suggested that some might be too young to bear testimony to Jesus.

Listen to what God says He has done for you, and then begin to speak and act for God.

We all must speak for Jesus,
   Who hath redemption wrought,
Who gave us peace and pardon,
   Which by His blood He bought.
We all must speak for Jesus,
   To show how much we owe
To Him who died to save us
   From death and endless woe.

We all must speak for Jesus,
   The aged and the young,
With manhood's fearless accents—
   With childhood's lisping tongue.
We all must speak for Jesus,
   His people far and near, —
The rich and poor on land or wave;
   The peasant and the peer.

We all must speak for Jesus,
   Where'er our lot may fall,
To brothers, sisters, neighbours,
   In cottage and in hall.
We all must speak for Jesus,
   The world in darkness lies,
With Him against the mighty
   Together we must rise.

We all must speak for Jesus,
   'Twill ofttimes try us sore.
But streams of grace, to aid us,
   Into our hearts he'll pour.
We all must speak for Jesus,
   Till He shall come again,
Proclaim His glorious gospel,
   His crown and endless reign.

Judgment

Our Reward.

I DON'T think we can know we are saved till the judgment day.'

'But it matters very little what we think, for God says that His Bible was written, that we may *know* that we have eternal life ' (i John v. 13).

This is the answer to such a false and absurd statement; God's word was written that we might antedate the judgment day and know its issues now. Do you think that the Apostle Paul, after having been 1800 years with the Lord, is to stand at the judgment day to know whether he is saved or not? This is most evidently absurd. In John V. 20-30 we get the whole point settled by infinite wisdom. If you have not 'passed from death unto life' down here below, and are thus standing in the rank of those who 'shall not come into judgment,' you will be damned to all eternity. As the tree falls it lies. The godly man cries, 'Enter not into judgment with Thy servant, for in Thy sight shall no man living be justified ' (Psalm cxliii. 2). Through death and resurrection in Christ, as those who have been judged and justified, we are prepared for eternity. From the above mistake, however, some are often inclined to flee to another

'How can I be judged after I am saved?'

'But God says *we* must *all* appear before the judgment-seat of Christ that *every one* may receive the things done- in his body, according to that he hath done, wheth-er it be good or bad ' (2 Cor. V. 10), and this is the answer to such a statement. Per-fectly reconcilable are these two. We shall never be judged as to whether we arc saved or lost, but every deed we have done shall be judged, deeds we have forgot-ten, deeds we did not know we had done. Those who are in Christ shall rejoice to see all their rubbish burned. Only then shall they know what grace has done for them; then they shall receive their rewards. Those not in Christ shall be destroyed with their works. ' If the righteous scarcely be saved, where shall the ungodly and the sinner appear?' We are justified by faith; we are judged according to our works. Many, even Christians, forget this, and think that because, as to justification, judicial-ly our sins are blotted out, that therefore there will be no judgment. This is most unscriptural. We are saved as to our persons, but we must all appear before the judgment seat of Christ. Our every motive shall then receive its exact value. ' What manner of persons ought we to be? ' Is it not practical infidelity on this point that leads Christians often to be careless? Beware! God is not mocked: whatsoever a man sows that shall he also reap.

I. The Son of God Healing.

In the beginning of John v. we see the contrast between the quickening power of Jesus and the weakness of legal ordinance, in the history of the infirm man at the pool of Bethesda, who had the desire for health, but not the power to profit by the occasional means — the angel's visit. To will was present with him, but to perform he could not. How like a man under law: 'But what the law could not do, in that it was weak through the flesh,' God did in Jesus. Jesus came to the powerless one, and by His word cured him: 'Arise, take up thy bed and walk.' Strength came on the spot. Here is the life manifested now: God manifest in the flesh: *the Son of God.*

II. The Son of Man Rejected.

The Jews, thinking themselves far better than Jesus, sought to kill Him because He wrought on the Sabbath. He showed that God could not rest amid sin and misery, and that He and the Father were one. The Jews sought to kill Him. What a marvel! God manifest in the flesh could become the victim of man's hatred! The Creator submitted to be killed by the creature! Yes; for He was *the Son of Man.*

Jesus now shows them the whole truth concerning the matter. He was not anoth-er God, but in full union with the Father; did 'nothing of Himself (there cannot be

118

two independent supreme Beings), ' but what He seeth the Father do;' and there is nothing that the Father does which He does not show the Son. Christ speaks of Himself as God. He also speaks of Himself as in a position to do the Father's will, as the perfect servant who can he seen of men.

III. Jesus, The Quickener and Judge.

To show His glory in so doing, He speaks of two things (verses 21, 22): — 'He *quickeneth* whom He will;' and the Father hath 'committed all *judgment* unto the Son.' As Son of God He gives *life*; but as Son of Man he may be 'rejected,' 'disallowed,' 'disowned," despised,' 'dishonoured;' therefore, 'the Father judgeth no man, but hath committed *all judgment* unto the Son, that all (even His rejecters) should honour the Son, even as they honour the Father.' If we do not receive Him in grace, we must honour Him by being judged by Him; and all are divided into these two classes. Men have many distinctions in society—high and low, rich and poor, old and young, good, bad, indifferent, very good, very bad; but the great division of mankind before God is into those who have been *quickened* by Jesus, the Son of God, or who shall come into *judgment* under Jesus, the Son of Man. To which class do you belong.? There must be no mistake on this point, for a slip here is fatal for ever. God has. left no doubt about the means of knowing it. He has given us a perfect test by which we may know infallibly, emphasised by a double '*verily*' from the mouth of Incarnate Truth.

IV. Every Believer Hath Everlasting Life.

'Verily, verily, I say unto you, he that heareth My word, and believeth Him who sent me, *hath* everlasting life.' '*He* that heareth my word.' This is the word that brought order out of chaos, light out of darkness. This is the word that made myriads of stars revolve around their centres. This is the word that formed man and beast, and tree and rock, that formed ' the sea and the ' dry land.' This is the word that Jairus' daughter heard as she lay on her couch in the sleep of death. This is the word that the son of the weeping widow heard at Nain's gate, as he was being carried out on his bier. This is the word that Lazarus heard as he lay rotting in his tomb, and hearing, came forth a living man. Whosoever now hears that word, and trusts that Father who sent Jesus, by believing this life-giving word, ' hath everlasting life.' Anxious soul, you have often said. Would that I could see Him with these eyes, I would draw from Him one word that would give me life. Would that I could see Him walking past my door, I would rush out and grasp His robe and be healed, as the poor woman was who touched His garment. Yes, but is His word not the same now, and far more important to us?—that blessed Word which His Spirit of truth has written about Him, and whispers into your soul concerning Him? For say not in thine heart who shall ascend up into heaven to bring Christ down? He *has* come down; or who shall descend to the grave to bring Him up? He is risen, He is gone above. But His word is in thy mouth and in thy heart, and will it not satisfy you — His word, which is nigh to you, close to you, ' the word of salvation which we preach? ' ' Hear, and your soul shall live.' What a contradiction! Can metaphysics explain it? Can man's reason fathom it? Yet we believe it. Man's line is too short for man's need, but he that believeth *'hath everlasting life.'* It is not a life on probation (as Adam's, which could be lost), but everlasting life, Jesus' own life; for it is 'no longer I, but *Christ that liveth in me.'* It is not that he shall have, but 'hath.' It is not the promise of a future blessing after the last day, but the gift and present possession of *life now! Heareth, believeth, hath*: what a gospel for poor dead sinners! We need no longer wait at ' pools,' for Jesus has come down; no longer do we seek and are unable to find, for He has come 'to seek and to save' the lost. He has come to undertake for those that are 'without strength.' What dishonour then, can there be like doubting His ' WORD!' The devil says. *Dare you believe* such good news? The Holy Ghost says. *Dare you doubt it?* The devil says. It would be presumption to hear His word, as if it were for *you.* The Holy Ghost says that it is just for *you*, and it would be the highest presumption, and a resisting of Him, to stop your ears.

V. Beyond Death and Judgment Now.

Besides having *life*, he that 'heareth and believeth' has something more. 'He shall not come into *judgment*! (It is the same word in the Greek as at verse 22, and should be so translated.) Why? Because 'He is *passed from death unto life*!" The everlasting life that we in believing get is a life in resurrection: life in a risen Christ. What a wonderful truth from Jesus' own lips! ' Shall not come into judgment,' as touching my guilt, my sins, my standing as a living man descended from the first Adam, but reckoned as condemned, judged, dead, buried, and now alive ' unto God,' already in Christ, on resurrection ground. This in no way interferes with our appearance as Christians before the tribunal of Christ (i Cor. v.), for judgment concerning our actions as believers; where we shall get reward, according to the just judgment of our Lord and Master — a most blessed, solemn, and sanctifying thought; but it places the believer, as to his standing, on new ground, beyond the judgment of sin, beyond its doom, beyond his death, in a new life, in which he can now serve God, in which he can stand with joy at that tribunal. How different is God's religion from man's notions of it! Man thinks that God's religion is at best a mere preparation for death and judgment; whereas our blessed Teacher shews us, in this Sword of His, that it is a *life beyond death and beyond judgment!* Christian, stand up alive unto God. Start up from thy sleep a living man. Thou shalt not come into judgment, but art passed *from death unto life*. All hearers oi His word, who trust in Him, have this immunity, whether they realise it or not. Jesus' word has settled all, and it is blasphemy to doubt it. Have you heard Him speak? You may have heard men preach the gospel. Have you really heard good news for yourself from God Himself?

VI. The Two Hours.

Jesus in the fifth chapter of John points to two PERIODS in which His power would be manifested, and speaks of the two classes of people on whom that power would be displayed. ' The hour is coming, and now is, when the dead shall hear the voice of the *Son of God*, and they that hear shall live.' Man was dead spiritually by sin, he is dead in sin, and Jesus came and quickened him. The hour was then, and is

120

going on still, in which He is causing the dead to hear His voice and live. Thousands have been saved in this hour by hearing the voice of the Son of God. For the Father hath given Jesus as the Son of God manifested here in the flesh ' to have life in Himself;' 'for,' said John, 'the life was manifested, and we have seen it, and bear witness, and shew unto you that eternal life which was with the Father, and was manifested unto us.' But all do not wish to receive Him, all will not hear Him; the most part reject, disown, cast Him out. To meet this state of things, the Father ' hath given Him authority to execute judgment, because He is the *Son of Man.'*

' As '*Son of Man*,' He was despised and dishonoured; as 'Son of Man,' He shall claim His kingdom; as 'Son of Man,' He shall 'execute judgment upon His rejectors;' as 'Son of Man' all nations shall be gathered before Him for judgment; as ' Son of Man,' He shall break His foes with a rod of iron; as 'Son of Man,'. He shall 'reign in righteousness;' as 'Son of Man,' He shall sit on the ' great white throne,' and before Him shall stand, ' the dead, small and great.' Grace, love, mercy, pity, pardon, life, having all been rejected, what now is left but wrath, destruction, vengeance, judgment, death? 'The Son of Man' —Jesus of Nazareth — the King of the Jews, shall then be on the throne, not on the cross; and not in Hebrew and Greek and Latin only will this be known, but all men of every tongue shall honour Him as they honour the Father, and shall own as King of kings and Lord of lords this ' Son of Man.'

'Marvel not at this: for the hour is coming, in the which all that are in the graves shall hear His voice and shall come forth; they that have done good unto the resurrection of life, and they that have done evil unto the resurrection of judgment.' In the first hour, which has already lasted upwards of 1800 years, the dead in trespasses and sins have been getting life; the other hour is not yet come, but in it two things will happen. Those that have done good shall be quickened to a resurrection of life — the quickening work of the Son of God being then, and not till then, perfectly completed — He being 'the Omega,' as well as 'the Alpha.' Those that have done evil shall also be raised, but to a resurrection of judgment — which, in their case shall certainly be eternal damnation. The whole line of thoughts is judgment (it is the same word as in verses 22 and 24), a judgment not of two Gods but of the one God, who has but one mind, one will, one judgment, though acting in different persons. All men, saved or lost, shall rise, because Christ is risen.

Reader, in which resurrection wilt thou share, that of life or of judgment? Wilt thou listen to the ' Son of God,' or dost thou await the judgment of the ' Son of Man?' Now is the time of passing from off the judgment ground through thy death into His life. There will be no change after thy spirit has left thy body. *Now,* this moment, as thou readest this line, pause and ask, Have I passed from death unto life? If not, hear His voice at this moment; believe His Father's love-message, whilst thou hearest 'His word,' 'God so loved the world" (' a term co-extensive with its rational and accountable generations') ' that He gave his only begotten Son, that whosoever' (of all the dead, ruined, God-hating sinners in it) ' believeth in Him should not perish, but have everlasting life,' 'This man receiveth *sinners*,' 'a designation that misses no one individual of the species.' That thou art not already in hell is due only to the tolerance of that God against whom thou daily sinnest. This is the hour of grace, of life, of pardon: the next hour must be the hour of vengeance, of judgment, of wrath. Sooner or later thou wilt know these *realities.* If you get into heaven at all, it must be by hearing His word and believing Him. Then, why not now? Are you afraid of making sure of being in heaven too soon? It is heaven on earth, if you knew it, to be *alive in a living Christ*, Why not antedate your heaven by beginning it now, even if you knew your hour would lengthen out ever so long? 'In Christ all are made alive.' But what a difference in the doom of the two classes who are made alive by Him! One is made alive because His Spirit dwells in them, the other because He is the powerful judge that condemns them to the lake of fire for ever.

VII. The Book Closed and Opened.

In Isa. Ixi. i, we read, 'The Spirit of the Lord God is upon me, because the Lord hath anointed me to preach good tidings unto the meek. He hath sent me to bind up the broken-hearted, to proclaim liberty to the captives, and the opening of the prison to the bound. To proclaim the **Acceptable Year of The Lord**, and the *day of vengeance of our God*. And in Luke iv, 18, when Jesus in the synagogue applied this to Himself, He finishes with 'the acceptable year of the Lord.' He does not go on to say, ' the day of vengeance of our God;' but it is written, ' He closed the book, and He gave it again to the minister, and sat down.' What a gospel is in that omission! On it has been hung the forbearance of these eighteen centuries. What love, what long-suffering, is in that word, '*He closed the book*,' that book which spoke of vengeance. The proclamation in this hour is, 'the acceptable year of the Lord'—grace, life from the Son of God; but what a day that will be when the book is opened, 'the day of vengeance of our God,' the execution of the judgment of the Son of Man!

In Rev. V. we see the acceptable year has revolved, the redeemed, worshipping, praising elders are gathered around Himself, and now the book is brought forward, and one of the elders says, ' Behold the lion of the tribe of Juda, the root of David, hath prevailed to *open the book*, and to loose the seven seals thereof This is the book of terrible wrath, the opening of the seals of which inaugurates fearful judgment upon a Christ-rejecting world. Wilt thou be under the vials of wrath, or wilt thou hear of life? 'The book' is closed as yet. He has handed it to His servants; He has left them to proclaim His grace. His gospel, and He has *sat down* waiting till His enemies are made His footstool. What a gospel! A closed book of vengeance, an open heaven, a preached gospel, a seated Christ, life from the Son of God! What a day is coming! An open book of wrath, the door of mercy shut, no more room, a risen Christ, judgment executed by the Son of Man!

Let me, in conclusion, place before you the teaching of Scripture concerning judgment as to a believer. There is,

1st, The Judgment of Sin.

This was at Calvary when Christ stood in the place of the sinner, putting away sin by the sacrifice of Himself He was made sin for us, bare our sins in His own body on the tree, was wounded for our transgressions, was bruised for our iniquities, when God laid our iniquities on Him. This was when He cried, 'My God, My God, why hast Thou forsaken Me?' That was for us. When we believe in Him this judgment can never alight on us. If we reject Him, this will be our doom in an eternal hell. It is this judgment spoken of in the passage above that the believer is beyond. He is no longer a convict. He is a son. He has not to meet the sentence of a judge. He is under the authority and discipline of his Father, and as such he will be judged; but how great the difference! He will not be judged to see whether he is a convict or a son; he will be judged as a son, for there is,

2d, The Judgment-seat of Christ.

'We must all appear before the judgment-seat of Christ.' Every Christian will render his account of everything he has done, every vain and idle word, every idle action, every deceit he has practised. Christian merchant, every trick of trade will then appear. Christian lady, every little polite He will appear then. When that lady came to see you yesterday, you remarked when you saw her coming, ' Oh! here is that disagreeable person, I wonder she comes here; ' and when you went into your drawing-room, with a smile you said to her, 'Oh! I'm so glad to see you.' — And you were not. — It was a lie.

Every one will suffer loss in as far as he has acted against his Lord's mind. Be ye holy for I am holy. Nothing will stand then but that which has proceeded from the new nature which is holy. Our wisdom, in prospect of that day of rewards, is to starve the old man and feed the new; to mortify the members which are upon the earth; to reproduce Christ in our daily life, since we have received Christ our everlasting life; to walk in the exhibition of that grace and truth which we have received; to *adorn* (we cannot make it true or false, but we can adorn) the doctrine of God our Saviour in all things.

Take care that you do not suffer loss in that day. In i Thess. iv. we find it will be when we are caught up out of this world to meet the Lord in the air. But the saint will be *glorified* when he reaches that tribunal, and one of his highest joys will be to see all his selfish works burned up, and all that was for God placed on his crown of righteousness. The crown of *gold* belongs to all the saints, for that is what Christ is, but the crown of *righteousness* is the righteous reward given to each according to his individual faithfulness. May we be using this world so as to gain this crown. May we now, as those not of the world, be packing up our goods and sending them on before. *Grace* has saved us and placed us beyond judgment; *truth* will give exact rewards to us as sons when we shall be openly acknowledged and acquitted in that day of judgment, and made perfectly blessed in the full enjoying of God to all eternity. And then, in the endless ages, the eternal day of God, when God is all and all, we shall be the brightest specimens of the righteousness and truth of God, and we shall also show in these ages to come ' the exceeding riches of His grace.'

Grace and truth came by Jesus Christ.

Grace and truth are now preached and exhibited in the conversion and walk of the Christian.

Grace and truth shall be fully manifested, and their power fully known to us as the glorified of the Lord, only at the glorious tribunal of Christ, and then for evermore.

Stand up from among the dead, and patiently work as one waiting for the judgment-seat of Christ.

123

'Tis first the true and then the beautiful,
  Not first the beautiful and then the true;
First the wild moor with rock, and reed, and pool,
  Then the gay garden rich in scent and hue.

'Tis first the good and then the beautiful,
  Not first the beautiful and then the good;
First the rough seed sown in the rougher soil,
  Then the flower blossom or the branching wood.

Not first the glad and then the sorrowful,
  But first the sorrowful and then the glad;
Tears for a day: for earth of tears is full,
  Then we forget that we were ever sad.

Not first the bright, and after that the dark,
  But first the dark, and after that the bright;
First the thick cloud, and then the rainbow's arc,
  First the dark grave, then resurrection light.

'Tis first the night — stern night of storm and war,
  Long night of heavy clouds, and veiled skies;
Then the far sparkle of the Morning Star,
  That bids the saints awake, and dawn arise.

Made in the USA
Coppell, TX
29 October 2023

23573359R00074